FAMILY VALUES

BY DAVID WILLIAMSON

CURRENCY PRESS
The performing arts publisher

GRIFFIN
THEATRE
COMPANY

CURRENT THEATRE SERIES

First published in 2020
by Currency Press Pty Ltd,
PO Box 2287, Strawberry Hills, NSW, 2012, Australia
enquiries@currency.com.au
www.currency.com.au
in association with Griffin Theatre Company

Typeset by Dean Nottle for Currency Press.
Cover image shows Andrew McFarlane. Cover photograph by Brett Boardman.
Cover design by Alphabet Studios.

A catalogue record for this
book is available from the
NATIONAL
LIBRARY
OF AUSTRALIA
National Library of Australia

Contents

Currency Press acknowledges the Traditional Owners of the Country on which we live and work. We pay our respects to all Aboriginal and Torres Strait Islander Elders, past and present.

For Kristen, who has been the inspiration for my strongest, most engaging female characters for many decades.

Family Values was first produced by Griffin Theatre Company at SBW Stables Theatre, Darlinghurst, on 17 January 2020, with the following cast:

SUE	Belinda Giblin
LISA	Danielle King
ROGER	Andrew McFarlane
MICHAEL	Jamie Oxenbould
EMILY	Ella Prince
NOELINE	Bishanyia Vincent
SABA	Sabryna Walters

Director, Lee Lewis
Dramaturg, Van Badham
Designer, Sophie Fletcher
Lighting Designer, Benjamin Brockman
Composer and Sound Designer, Steve Francis
Stage Manager, Khym Scott

CHARACTERS

ROGER COLLINS, 70, retired judge
SUE, his wife
LISA, 42, their daughter
MICHAEL, their son
EMILY, their daughter
NOELINE, Emily's partner
SABA NAZARI, 27, Iranian

SETTING

Roger and Sue's living room.

ROGER, *70, stands alone by a dining room table already laid out with drinks and snacks for an imminent gathering. He's trying to tie the neck of a coloured balloon to prevent the air from escaping. His fingers are not as nimble as they used to be so he's finding it difficult. So far he has only managed to tie the necks of two balloons which rest on the table. A pile of uninflated balloons lie waiting.*

SUE *enters from the kitchen and watches his inept efforts. She can't stand it any longer and steps up and starts to blow up and tie the other balloons much more efficiently.* ROGER *is relieved and starts to tie the inflated balloons together on a piece of string.*

ROGER: Stupid idea.

SUE: You wanted it.

ROGER: No. Not the birthday gathering. The balloons.

SUE: They were your idea too.

ROGER: I thought it would bring back fond memories of *their* parties. But all I can remember is shouting and chaos.

SUE: You used to head straight for your office.

ROGER: You were better with discipline.

SUE: I had to be, didn't I? Your idea of discipline was to clear your throat and frown.

ROGER: Are you sure I fathered them?

      SUE *stares at him.*

It *was* the seventies. [*He shrugs.*] How can they possibly share the same gene pool? Michael and Lisa? And Emily?

SUE: What's wrong with Emily?

ROGER: Suddenly for no apparent reason she turns her whole life around. Are *you* happy with her new partner?

SUE: A little too forceful for my liking.

ROGER: I meant … gender.

SUE: It was a surprise but I'm getting used to it.

ROGER: I'm damned if I am. And to make it worse her name's Noeline.

SUE: What's wrong with Noeline?

ROGER: Every Noeline I've ever met has been … strident. And this one's no exception.

SUE: Try and be nice to her.

ROGER: [*staring at* SUE *in horror*] She's not coming? I thought you were supposed to make sure—

SUE: She insisted.

ROGER: On what grounds?

SUE: She's made it clear to Emily that if they're going to marry she expects to be accepted as one of the family.

ROGER: I don't want her as part of the family.

SUE: Short of murder, it's about to happen. For God's sake, don't tell her how you voted.

ROGER: She knows.

SUE: How?

ROGER: Emily asked me if I was voting yes. I told her I may be old-fashioned but I still believe marriage should be between a man and a woman.

SUE: The yes vote does still allow that to happen.

ROGER: How do all those trendy 'yes' voters feel now as their wives leave them and marry women.

SUE: [*incredulous*] What?

ROGER: It's happening. I read it.

SUE: Where? Miranda Devine?

ROGER: Some of what she says makes sense.

SUE: That's grounds for divorce.

ROGER: Emily's marriage was perfectly fine. What was wrong with Neville?

SUE: He's the only anaesthetist in Sydney who doesn't need drugs to put his patients to sleep.

ROGER: Okay, Neville can drone on a bit, but to dump him for a pit bull like Noeline? I just don't get the attraction?

SUE: Apparently Neville never worked out his penis wasn't just for urination.

ROGER: Sex? It's about sex?

SUE: When you haven't had it for six years it's a plausible reason.

ROGER: She likes it better with … Noeline?

SUE: She says unlike your average man, women know what to do with each other.

ROGER: So I guess you're about to leave me for that chiropodist of yours.

SUE: She's made an approach and I'm considering it.

ROGER *stares at her.*

That was what's called a 'joke'.

ROGER: I know what a joke is.

SUE: You've never made one, so I didn't like to assume.

ROGER: Don't you worry about little Phoebe and Josh? Their mother out on the ocean most of the year? We get to see them more than she does.

SUE: They seem happy with Neville.

ROGER: All children deserve to have a father and a mother.

SUE: Ours only got a mother.

ROGER: That's rubbish!

SUE: Ask them. Their most frequent memory is a closed office door which they knew they couldn't enter because [*in a hushed tone*] 'Daddy is working on a judgement'.

ROGER: The court was overloaded.

SUE: Lisa's teacher told her all judgements came from heaven. She thought you were God.

ROGER: That didn't last long.

SUE: Don't try and deny I did the lion's share of bring them up.

ROGER: My workload—

SUE: I had a punishing workload too. As a social worker you have to manage human distress at the coalface, not juggle legal abstractions.

ROGER: I was earning a lot more than you. Laying the financial foundation for the life we lead now.

SUE: The life we lead now includes three children who grew up thinking they weren't important enough to warrant your attention.

ROGER: So how come I was the one they came to when you wouldn't listen to them?

SUE: They knew I wouldn't indulge them.

ROGER: I indulged them?

SUE: You were a soft touch.

ROGER: You were too tough on them sometimes.

SUE: I had eight hours a day of people with real problems. I wasn't going to put up with petty whinges.

ROGER: They weren't always petty whinges.

SUE: When you did finally emerge to do a bit of fathering, you patted them on the head and told them they were wonderful, totally undermining my efforts to edge them towards maturity.

ROGER: Happy birthday Roger.

SUE: Sorry. You triggered a few old resentments.

ROGER: Is there some way I can avoid triggering any more?

SUE: [*with a sigh*] You're a dear thing most of the time—

ROGER: I have some good qualities?

SUE: You're kind, you're generous, but some gremlin snap-froze your social attitudes sometime around 1959.

ROGER: Is there something wrong with being a social conservative?

SUE: Yes. It condemns everyone who's not powerful, white, heterosexual and male to feel they haven't got a voice.

ROGER: Turn on Radio National and all you hear are minority groups shrieking their grievances.

SUE: Thank God. Every other voice we hear is a paid lackey of Murdoch!

ROGER: You can browbeat me as much as you like but I don't like the fact that Emily is marrying a woman!

SUE: Well, it's happening, so when she arrives with Noeline, try and be a little gracious!

> LISA, *42, enters with* SABA, *27. She has overheard what her mother has just said.*

LISA: Noeline is coming?!

ROGER: Yes, she thinks of herself as one of the family.

LISA: We can't stay.

ROGER: You've just arrived.

LISA: Noeline's the captain of a Border Force cutter.

SUE: So?

LISA: Dad, Mum, this is Daniela. We're in a bit of an emergency situation. We're on the run.

SUE: On the run?

> LISA *takes out her iPhone and sends a quick text message.*

LISA: Border Force are hunting for her.

ROGER: Border Force?

LISA: Killcare. I need the keys. We need it for a couple of weeks.

SUE: What's going on?

SABA: I was brought here under the medevac laws.

LISA: And she's fled community detention.

ROGER: Why?

LISA: Gary Duckett is hell bent on sending her back to Nauru.

ROGER: But by fleeing you're just making matters worse.

SABA *starts to try and explain, but* LISA *cuts her off*

LISA: Dad, she's just had two psychiatric assessments saying she's at high risk of suicide if she was ever sent back to Nauru.

SUE: Then why is Duckett doing it?

LISA: He hates the fact that any refugees got here under the medevac laws. The prick!

ROGER: I wish you wouldn't use language like that about a democratically elected Minister of the Crown—

LISA: You think you're still living in a democracy?

ROGER: Of course we are. A democracy protected by the rule of law.

LISA: Yeah. Sixty-two new security laws in the last ten years.

ROGER: Lawfully enacted by an elected parliament.

SUE: Every one of them designed to curtail our freedom to act and speak.

ROGER: Enacted to respond to a worsening security situation.

SUE: Journalists raided because they were gutsy enough to tell us about appalling behaviour we've got an absolute right to know about! Is that what should happen in a democracy?

ROGER: Susan, I don't think it's fruitful at this moment to enter into this debate. [*To* LISA] All I want to know is why are you involved?

LISA: We were alerted when Daniela escaped and I've been assigned to hide her.

ROGER: We? Who's we?

LISA: You don't need to know.

SUE: If you're wanting to hide her in our holiday house, perhaps we do.

LISA: You don't need to know.

ROGER: Do you realise the consequences of what you're doing?

LISA: Yes.

SUE: What's happening to Daniela sounds awful, but did you have to do this on your father's birthday?

LISA: I'm the only one in my group without any known links to her that Border Force can trace.

SABA: I'm sorry to disrupt this special occasion, Justice Collins. I really am.

LISA: Call him Mr Collins. He's retired.

ROGER: Most people still accord me the respect of Justice.

LISA: Dad, this is scarcely the situation for formalities.

SABA: I'm happy to call your father Justice Collins.

SUE: Don't you dare. He's retired. He can learn to be human again.

LISA: Dad, I need the keys to Killcare.

ROGER: Hasn't anyone told you harbouring an illegal resident is a criminal offence?

LISA: Ten years jail or a fine of 180,000 dollars or both, but what our government is doing is nothing short of barbarous.

SABA: I can't go back there, Justice Collins.

ROGER: I understand your distress, Daniela, but I can't possibly be party to a serious offence.

LISA: I'm committing the offence.

ROGER: I give you those keys and I'm aiding and abetting it.

SUE: She can say she had a copy of the key. Nobody will know.

ROGER: I'll know, and if I'm questioned I won't perjure myself. [*To* SABA] Surely it can't be that bad on Nauru. You're housed, you're fed, you're free to travel anywhere on the island. Gary Duckett said you're all buying Armani jeans.

SABA: [*indicating her jeans*] I wish. Target. Twelve dollars.

LISA: Dad, you can't possibly believe anything Gary Duckett says!

ROGER: I know he's the object of derision as far as you inner-city, latte-sipping, deep green—

SUE: Roger, please don't keep stereotyping your daughter as a latte-sipping—

ROGER: And she doesn't stereotype me?

SUE: You deserve it.

LISA: As do all the other aging Anglo males desperately clinging on to the power and privileges they've unfairly appropriated.

ROGER: You're trying to tell me you haven't been privileged? Educated at huge expense at a school where you walk in the gates and encounter such manicured arboreal perfection that you half expect a heavenly choir to pop out from behind the privet hedge and welcome you to the afterlife?

LISA: I got privileges I didn't deserve—

ROGER: So you've now devoted your life to making sure nobody else does.

LISA: Dad, I need the Killcare keys.

SUE: Give her the keys, Roger.

ROGER: No! We finally get to the part of life when we can relax, travel and enjoy ourselves. I'm not risking ten years jail.

SUE: Where are the keys!

ROGER: She's already put us in an invidious position. Right now, according to the law, we should be phoning Border Force and reporting an illegal fugitive.

SUE: You do that and it's divorce.

LISA: Don't even think of it, Dad!

SUE: Roger. I've put up with your views for years, but if you turn that girl in—

ROGER: Darling, if I don't I'm complicit!

LISA: Dad, I can't begin to tell you how badly Saba's been treated.

ROGER: Saba?

SABA: Saba is my real name. Daniela is just a cover.

LISA: It took three urgent medical requests and two suicide attempts, the last one almost successful, before Saba made it here for psychiatric treatment.

ROGER: If Duckett thinks she's had sufficient treatment, he's got the right to send her back.

LISA: Two expert and independent psychiatric assessments made just over a week ago both agreed Saba was still at high risk of suicide if she's returned. Duckett ignored them and was doing everything in his power to get her back to Nauru.

SABA: Read the reports yourself, Justice Collins.

She delves in her bag and hands them to him. He takes them.

ROGER: [*indicating the reports*] If they're that bad I find it hard to believe Duckett would be that callous.

SUE: Gary Duckett bites the head off a kitten every morning to get himself prepared for the day.

ROGER: When he appears on television it is hard to suppress an involuntary shudder, but to be fair to the man he's trying to ensure no more refugees will be drowned at sea.

LISA: Dad, come on. You know this has very little to do with saving refugees from drowning.

SUE: The real reason is to keep as many Muslims as possible out of Australia.

ROGER: That's your assumption.

SUE and LISA [*together*] Oh migod!

SABA: The irony is I'm secular. The mullahs forced us to wear a hijab but they couldn't force me what to think.

LISA: Our country should have welcomed Saba, not kept her for years on a godforsaken Pacific hellhole.

ROGER: A bolshy wife, a Get Up daughter. What have I done to deserve this?

SUE: You think it's been fun for me to wake up every morning beside a doppelganger of Cory Bernadi?

ROGER: I can't risk breaking the law after a lifetime of upholding it.

SUE: Where are the keys?

ROGER: I'm not about to tell you.

SUE: I'll find them.

ROGER: No you won't.

LISA: Dad, we have to be out of here before Noeline arrives.

SUE: Don't worry, love. We'll find them. He hasn't the creativity to find a good hiding place.

ROGER: Thank you.

> SUE *is just about to leave with* LISA *to search for the keys when* MICHAEL *enters through the open front door carrying a parcel.*

MICHAEL: Happy birthday, Dad.

ROGER: Thanks, son.

> ROGER *takes the present.*

SUE: [*kissing him*] Glad you could make it. You're looking very well.

MICHAEL: And have been ever since I allowed the Lord to enter my soul.

> *He looks defiantly at his sister* LISA *as he says it.*

[*Indicating the present*] It's a box set of DVDs of our most popular songs of worship. [*Defiantly to both* LISA *and* SUE] I defy anyone to listen to those and not feel something stir inside.

LISA: Nausea.

ROGER: Lisa, don't bait your brother. The last thing I need on my seventieth is a re-run of the near lethal hostility we've endured between you two for twenty years!

MICHAEL: [*looking at* SABA *with a disapproving frown*] So, hello. I'm Michael. You are?

SABA, LISA and SUE: [*together*] Daniela.

MICHAEL: And Daniela? Your reason for celebrating my father's birthday?

LISA: Daniela's a close friend.

MICHAEL: I understood this was family only. If I'd been told otherwise I would have brought a close friend of mine. Monica.

SUE: Who's Monica?

MICHAEL: A lovely Christian mother of four I've formed a friendship with.

SUE: Mother of four?

MICHAEL: Why the tone of disapproval?

SUE: You've got children of your own.

MICHAEL: Who I rarely see due to my ex-wife's vindictiveness. When I found the Lord I hoped Deidre and the kids would follow, but it wasn't to be and I've accepted that it's all part of the Lord's plan.

LISA: Your divorce was part of the Lord's plan?

MICHAEL: He plans all lives.

LISA: If you're struck down by cancer, or fail to see an oncoming bus, it's because he likes to spring a surprise or two?

ROGER: Lisa. Michael has his beliefs, you have yours.

MICHAEL: Thank you, Dad.

SUE: [*to* LISA] Yes, let's see if we can all be a little more tolerant.

MICHAEL: So, Daniela. A close friend?

LISA: Yes she is.

MICHAEL: She must be to be here on a family only occasion.

LISA: Daniela and I work together helping refugees resettle. We've got a strategy meeting to get to. Dad, just give us the keys to Killcare and Sa—Daniela and I will go.

MICHAEL: A strategy meeting? At Killcare?

LISA: We've got a lot of issues to work through.

MICHAEL: How long have you been here? Half an hour?

LISA: We're just dropping in.

MICHAEL: Just dropping in. On your father's seventieth birthday?

SUE: Michael, stop this.

MICHAEL: I'm sorry, Mum, but none of this is making any sense. You could surely hold your strategy meeting at your flat, at a cafe or anywhere?

LISA: The issues are difficult. We need to concentrate. Dad, the keys please?

ROGER: You're not having them.

LISA: Dad!

SUE: Roger!

MICHAEL: You come here, spend a few minutes with your father on his seventieth, demand the use of his holiday house, and when he says no, you get petulant. Find a cafe!

LISA: Dad, the keys. Please. You know why we need them.

MICHAEL: Dad, give them the keys. It's always better when she's not around.

ROGER: I can't. They don't want to go to Killcare just for—

SUE: Roger, that's enough.

MICHAEL: Enough about what?

ROGER: Daniela is—

LISA: Dad! Stop it. [*Indicating* MICHAEL] His politics are even further to the right than yours!

MICHAEL: My politics? What is this all about?

ROGER: Daniela is—

LISA: [*to* ROGER] Dad, no!

MICHAEL: What are you trying to hide?

> LISA *frantically tries to summon up a convincing lie.*

LISA: Okay, let's not have any secrets. Daniela and I are an item. And we all know what you think about that.

ROGER: Lisa, it's not— [necessary to]

LISA: Dad. Keep quiet.

SABA: An item? What is an item?

MICHAEL: Not just one of my sisters, but two! [*To his parents*] You accept this? Another Sapphic pairing in the family.

SABA: [*the penny drops*] Sapphic.

LISA: Forget it. Ignore whatever he says. He's mad. [*To* MICHAEL] You know the facts now, so leave it at that.

MICHAEL: Why would you be worried that I'd tell anyone? Don't you all love to shout it to the world these days?

LISA: Daniela's parents are conservative. We're keeping it very quiet at the moment. Can we leave it at that?

MICHAEL: Well no. I won't. You are flagrantly violating God's law and I'm free to tell you just what I think of that.

SUE: Michael, enough!

MICHAEL: You can shut down Israel Folau but you won't shut down me. [*To his parents*] You both think that what Emily and now Lisa are doing is okay?

SUE: Yes.

ROGER: No.

MICHAEL: Dad, stick to your guns.

LISA: [*to* ROGER] Please. The keys. It's urgent.

MICHAEL: The urgency of your lust somehow overrides your father's moral objections?

LISA: Dad!

MICHAEL: [*to* ROGER] Dad, don't let her bully you. Our Saviour is up there applauding you.

LISA: You idiot!

ROGER: Lisa!

MICHAEL: [*to* LISA] What you do with your body is up to your own conscience, but you have no right to try and force Dad—

SUE: Michael, stop this! You were a half-reasonable human being before you fell in with those preening, prancing yodelling nut cases at Hillsong.

ROGER: Sue.

MICHAEL: I'm a nut case?

SUE: [*to* ROGER] I love our son, but that doesn't mean I have to love what he's become.

MICHAEL: You'd prefer I was still leading a life without purpose or meaning. Someone who filled the void with senseless obsessions.

SUE: Frankly yes. Roger, please. The keys.

ROGER: No.

SUE: [*to* LISA] We're just going to have to find the bloody things.

LISA *and* SUE *disappear in the direction of the bedrooms.*

ROGER: You're being too hard on yourself, son. Your matchstick models were not senseless. The Taj Mahal was quite special.

MICHAEL: The hardest was the Colosseum. All the wrecked bits.

ROGER: They were all great.

MICHAEL: Thanks, Dad.

ROGER: The Eiffel Tower. How many hours went into that?

MICHAEL: Nearly two hundred. But Deidre probably had a point. Building an extra room to house them all *was* excessive.

ROGER: I really liked it. You went in there and came out feeling like you'd just been on a world tour.

MICHAEL: Without the hassle of airports and customs. Exactly.

ROGER: You needn't apologise for them.

MICHAEL: Thanks, Dad. I've always been grateful for your encouragement.

By this stage SABA *has sunk into a trance on the sofa.*

ROGER: [*going across and sitting next to* SABA] If I could possibly help I would, but you have to realise what you're asking—

SABA: I didn't want this to happen, Justice Collins.

MICHAEL: My sister seduced you?

ROGER: Michael, please, just relax. Relax.

MICHAEL: Daniela, it's obvious you're regretting what you've done and regret is the pathway to redemption. Let the Lord enter your heart and you will know the joys of eternal life.

SABA *looks at him with bewilderment. She goes to join* SUE *and* LISA.

I think she can be saved.

ROGER *sits almost in a catatonic trance himself. He struggles to find something to say.*

ROGER: On reflection, I think I liked your Parthenon the best.

MICHAEL: Yes, me too, but Mum's right. All that model making was a waste of my life.

ROGER: It gave you a lot of pleasure.

MICHAEL: Dad, life isn't about pleasure. If we worship God, work hard and aspire, He will gift us our reward.

ROGER: Which is?

MICHAEL: Health and wealth. The Catholic fetishisation of the poor and the wretched is a self-flagellating perversion of our Lord's positive message. Jesus didn't want us to be poor.

ROGER: 'Blessed are the meek, for they shall inherit the earth'?

MICHAEL: 'I wish above all things that thou mayest prosper and be in health.' 3 John, 1:2. Dad, I know you have reservations about my new direction, but I'm part of a warm, vibrant and loving community who value me. Lisa can sneer all she likes, but for the first time in my life I'm truly happy.

ROGER: I'm glad to hear that, son. Knowing that your child is happy is the best thing that can ever happen to a parent.

MICHAEL: My biggest hope, deep down, is that you and Mum will find the Lord too, before it's too late.

ROGER: Ah.

MICHAEL: I want you to be there with me in heaven.

ROGER: That's very nice of you, Michael.

MICHAEL: Well, if I'm truthful, particularly you. It's a little un-Christian of me to have favourites, but I know that I've always been a little— different. And you've always been more tolerant of that than Mum.

ROGER: Your mother loves you as much as I do.

MICHAEL: Yes, but she was always … crabby with us. Particularly me.

ROGER: In fairness to your mother, I was missing in action a lot of the time.

MICHAEL: I know I've never been easy. A tendency to be a little …

ROGER: You were fine.

MICHAEL: … a little on the obsessive side.

ROGER: Maybe just a—

MICHAEL: The football cards. The Lego. Collecting—

MICHAEL and ROGER: Autographs—

ROGER: You had your hobbies.

MICHAEL: I have whole books full of illegible scrawls from Big Brother contestants everybody's long since forgotten.

Beat.

And it irritated Mum, I know it did, but you were always—

ROGER: Your mother—

MICHAEL: —tolerant, encouraging.

ROGER: Well, thank you, but—

MICHAEL: When I joined Hillsong you were the only one in the family who approved. And now, in under two years, I've become the new chair of the doctrinal disputes committee.

ROGER: And you'd be very good at it.

MICHAEL: I didn't get to be chief building compliance officer for Sydney's fourth-largest council without the ability to grasp complex regulations.

ROGER: And the personality to enforce them.

MICHAEL: Since the Lord entered my heart I'm much more lenient. I now understand developers as hard-working contributors to our national wellbeing.

ROGER: Ah.

MICHAEL: There are quite a few amongst our number. And they're very generous with their contributions.

ROGER: Ah.

> EMILY *enters with* NOELINE.

EMILY: Happy birthday, Dad.

NOELINE: Happy birthday, Mr Collins. We brought you a present.

ROGER: Not necessary. But thanks.

> *He takes the package* NOELINE *hands him and starts to unwrap it. It's a book with rainbow colours on the cover.*

NOELINE: It's the story of the long fight for marriage equality in pictures.

ROGER: Ah, thank you, Noeline. Emily.

NOELINE: I know you two voted no, which I do find, I have to be honest, deeply upsetting.

MICHAEL: It's Dad's birthday!

EMILY: Noels—

NOELINE: Birthdays were no cause for celebration for me, Michael. Another year of living a lie. Another year of guilt and self-hatred. So excuse me if I feel it necessary to confront this honestly and make it clear that the 'vote no' campaign caused me, and others like me, intense pain.

EMILY: Noels, it's Dad's birthday.

NOELINE: Ems, I did warn you that if I came today I had no intention of pulling any punches.

ROGER: And you certainly aren't. Is it possible a little wine might have a … mellowing effect? I'd be very happy to pour your some.

NOELINE: The sarcasm's unnecessary, Mr Collins. I'll pour my own wine.

> *She goes across to the opened bottles of wine and pours some for herself and* EMILY.

EMILY: Noels, I'd prefer the white.

NOELINE: It's chardonnay. You don't like chardonnay. I'll pour you some red. [*Tasting*] No. Too heavy. Shiraz soup. [*To* ROGER] Would you have any pinot?

ROGER: Yes, it's in the rack over there.

>*He gets up to get it, but* NOELINE *gets it herself, unscrews it, pours and tastes.*

NOELINE: Better. I'll pour you some, Ems.

EMILY: Maybe I'll just try the chardonnay first.

NOELINE: You hate chardonnay and this is a very drinkable pinot.

EMILY: Okay. Pour me some pinot.

>EMILY *accepts the pinot* NOELINE *puts in her hands, then quaffs it with the air of someone who desperately needs some dulling alcohol in her system.*

ROGER: That's a lovely dress you're wearing, Emily.

NOELINE: I know what suits her.

ROGER: Right.

>*Awkward pause.*

NOELINE: Sorry. I didn't mean to come on quite that strong. I apologise.

ROGER: Thank you.

NOELINE: But the fact is that I'm deeply in love with your daughter and I hope for her sake you can come to terms with that.

EMILY: Noels!

NOELINE: Ems, I'd like your father to try and understand. [*To* ROGER] I was an emotional cot case until I met Emily. I was coping with my job, in fact better than coping, I was excelling, but inside I was empty. Totally empty. Then your daughter joined Border Force and from the minute I saw her I loved her. I thought it could never happen because it's breaking all rules to let anything start between a Commanding Officer and one of my crew. I tried hard to suppress it, but to my joy and amazement Emily felt it too, and finally it became a mutual passion we couldn't deny. This is real for both of us, Mr Collins. I need you to know that.

ROGER: Noeline, I appreciate your honesty and sincerity, and while yes, this is hard for me to accept, if Emily is happy then I'm happy for her.

>NOELINE *hesitates, a little tearful, then suddenly and impulsively hugs him. He's startled.*

NOELINE: Thank you. [*Turning to* MICHAEL] I do hope eventually you can see things like your father.

MICHAEL: No I can't. You're breaking God's law.

NOELINE: Human happiness is far more important than appeasing you and your medieval world view.

MICHAEL: Faith? That's what you call faith?

ROGER: Noeline, I've tried to be as tolerant to your world view. Could you also try and tolerate the beliefs of my son?

NOELINE: Faith? Another name for anti-gay bigotry?

MICHAEL: So this is the new shape of the family? Noeline is allowed to express beliefs which are deeply offensive to me ad nauseam, but if I dare mention the joy the Lord has brought to me it's a total no-no.

ROGER: That does appear to be the new reality.

MICHAEL: I refuse to be the designated outsider in my own family.

EMILY: Michael, just shut up!

ROGER: [*angry*] Can we please have a modicum of tolerance here?! You've got very different views of life. Accept it please and move on.

MICHAEL: Move on to where, Dad? Marriage between man and pig?

EMILY: Michael.

MICHAEL: And churches forced by politically correct laws to officiate?

ROGER: Michael, push it to absurdity and you destroy your own credibility!

EMILY: He did that long ago.

ROGER: [*really upset*] Enough! Both of you. Enough!

MICHAEL: [*to* EMILY] You'll be delighted to hear that your sister has also become a roger dodger.

EMILY: What?

MICHAEL: Lisa and her new female 'friend' can't wait to flee to their Killcare love nest.

EMILY: Lisa? The same Lisa who so proudly claimed she had bedded seven Justins, six Jasons and two Josephs in one calendar year?

MICHAEL: She obviously ran out of men and has had to look elsewhere. Ah, speak of the devil.

> LISA, SUE *and* SABA *enter.* EMILY *stares at* SABA.

EMILY: Well, you are a dark horse. Are you going to introduce me to your … er … lovely new friend …

LISA: Daniela, this is my sister Emily, and her partner Noeline. They both work for Border Force.

SABA: Yes, you told me.

LISA: [*underlining it as a warning*] Noeline is the Commanding Officer of a Border Force high-speed cutter.

SABA: Yes, you told me.

LISA: They intercept boatfuls of refugees and board their vessels then send them back to refugee camps without hope in Indonesia, or to prison, torture or worse in Sri Lanka and Vietnam.

EMILY: I don't make our laws!

LISA: You just carry them out.

NOELINE: We're stopping refugee drownings at sea. And we're doing it with great efficiency and at considerable risk to ourselves. And I'm very proud of that fact.

LISA: Noeline, everyone with half a brain knows this policy is nothing to do with saving lives at sea. It's to reassure the western suburbs of Sydney that as many Muslims as possible are being stopped from reaching Australia.

ROGER: Lisa, lives are being saved.

LISA: A positive by-product of a Government pandering to Islamophobia.

EMILY: Noels it *is* partly about keeping out Muslims.

NOELINE: Ems if you don't believe in what we're doing, then perhaps you should reconsider your future.

SUE: Noeline, that sounded very much like you're threatening my daughter for merely expressing an opinion.

EMILY: Mum, please—

SUE: No. Someone who comes in here and demands to be accepted into a family then bullies and threatens one of its members is not someone I particularly want to be part of the family.

ROGER: Darling. Please. This is something they have to sort out.

SUE: My daughter is gay. Fine. She wants to get married. Fine. But she wants to get married to someone who tries to stop her saying what she thinks? Not fine.

EMILY: Mum, please.

NOELINE: You can't belong to an organisation and not adhere to its core beliefs.

LISA: Even when its core beliefs include forcibly sending legitimate refugees back to Nauru when their health is still in grave danger?

NOELINE: Refugee agitators hire lawyers who find tame doctors who make sure the treatment will go on forever.

SABA: [*angrily*] That's a lie.

NOELINE: And how can *you* be so sure of that?

LISA: Daniela works with me, helping refugees.

SUE: The very worst thing is to send someone who is psychologically distressed back to a place that will only make it worse.

NOELINE: Psychologically distressed? I can't see why being fed, clothed and looked after on Nauru would be any more stressful than what I have to do. Try commanding a vessel for eighty days in seas as treacherous as any in the world. Boarding vessels in seas like that. Don't talk to me about stress.

SUE: No-one doubts you're competent and brave, Noeline. But we're talking about the wisdom of sending vulnerable people back to a place where their condition can only get worse. What possible end does it serve?

NOELINE: Even if only a handful are allowed to stay here in Australia, the boats will start again. The smugglers will have a product to sell.

SABA: [*angrily*] And what exactly will they have to sell!

LISA: [*imitating a people smuggler*] 'Get on my boat and after six hellish years on Nauru, you just might be lucky enough to get so suicidal you'll be sent to Australia. They'll let you stay a couple of weeks then they'll send you back before your treatment is finished. And this will only cost you ten thousand dollars.' What a bargain!

NOELINE: Bend the rules and the boats will start again!

EMILY: [*to* NOELINE] Noeline, even if we let all the people on Manus and Nauru come here tomorrow, we'll still be out there stopping the boats.

NOELINE: We're just coping now! Triple the boats and they'd swamp us.

EMILY: Did you listen to Lisa? Six years of hell and they finally make it here? People smugglers can't sell that!

NOELINE: Emily, I'm your commanding officer and I know more about this than you do, so keep your opinions to yourself!

SUE: It's a perfectly legitimate opinion. Stand up for yourself, Emily.

LISA: She can't. Never has been able to.

EMILY: [*angry*] I just did! Are you deaf?!

> EMILY *retreats, stung by her sister's attack.*

NOELINE: What would *your* political pals do, Lisa? Disband Border Force? Let Muslims in by the thousands again? Welcome them as nice gentle people who have nothing to do with the terrorist outrages their comrades are unleashing on the world every second day?

SUE: There are a tiny minority of Muslims who are angry at the racism they experience and overreact.

LISA: Moderate Muslims abhor the use of violence.

MICHAEL: Moderate Muslims? Is there really such a thing? When the Twin Towers went down Muslims all over America had parties to celebrate.

LISA: That's an urban myth.

MICHAEL: I've seen the news footage. And don't get me started about ISIS.

NOELINE: Beheading Christians and laughing as they did it.

LISA: Brenton Tarrant slaughtered fifty-one Muslims in New Zealand and told the world he was a Christian crusader.

NOELINE: I'm not defending Christians either! Especially not after their hysterical 'vote no' campaign.

LISA: Christians and Muslims are two loopy sects kicked off by guys who heard voices in their head. These days we call them schizophrenics and give them treatment.

MICHAEL: Lisa, that's an appalling blasphemy.

ROGER: Lisa, stop it!

MICHAEL: She's always done it. She's not going to stop now.

NOELINE: [to LISA] Most Christians *are* anti-gay bigots, but Muslims are even worse. I'd be stoned to death for marrying your sister if we lived in Saudi Arabia or Iran.

LISA: That's not true.

SABA: It is, Lisa. Thousands of gay people have been executed in the past and it is still the law in Iran.

NOELINE: Daniela appears to be more abreast of reality than you, Lisa.

SABA: There are many regrettable things about the current regime's interpretations of the Quran.

NOELINE: [to LISA] I won't let you brand me as an ignorant Islamophobe who doesn't know what she's talking about. Since you brought up Iran, let's look at exactly what happens there. Women can vote but they are effectively barred from being parliamentarians or ever standing for President. They are barred from the judiciary and they are barred from travelling abroad unless their husbands permit it. Men can divorce women for any reason they choose.

LISA: That's not true—

SABA: It is.

NOELINE: After a divorce the father gets guardianship of the children. In courts the testimony of a man is given twice the weight of a woman's. Women are all forced to wear the hijab and if they protest they go to prison for years. And let's then go to the fact that women are barred or discouraged from entering many professions such as medicine—

LISA: No.

SABA: Yes. And women can be forced into marriage at thirteen years old, and must submit to sex and any other direction of their husbands or lose the remainder of their rights—

LISA: Which isn't right. I'm not saying it is.

ROGER: Lisa, we can't pretend they're not a threat. Paris. A hundred and thirty killed at a concert. The Madrid train bombing, a hundred and ninety-two killed. London, seven major terrorist attacks last year. Berlin, Christmas market attack. Nice, eighty-six innocent people mowed down.

LISA: Dad, the fact is that you're a hundred times more likely to die in a car accident in Europe than a terrorist attack! Security and surveillance are getting better and better. The Islamophobic scare campaign is just a hysterical overreaction to a relatively minor problem—

> *'Relatively minor' are trigger words for an angry and overlapping reaction. A verbal brawl erupts.*

MICHAEL: Relatively minor!

NOELINE: Relatively minor?!

SUE: Relatively—yes!

MICHAEL: I hope you feel like that when—

LISA: In Europe—a hundred times more likely to die in a road accident!

MICHAEL: —when you find yourself being shot at—

LISA: Latest figures!

MICHAEL: —being shot at with a high-velocity automatic—

LISA: Michael, you're being stupidly alarmist!

MICHAEL: —automatic weapon as you get off your train at Central Station one morning!

ROGER: Son, that's a little over the top.

LISA: Way over the top! It's always—

MICHAEL: Not really, Dad, I read it in the *Telegraph*.

LISA: —the same with— [Michael]

MICHAEL: It's probably being planned right now!

SUE: Read it in the *Telegraph*!

LISA: The *Telegraph*!

NOELINE: It almost certainly is being planned. Along with dozens of others.

EMILY: Noeline, that's over the top too!

MICHAEL: The Lindt Cafe! It's happened already!

LISA: Once, Michael, once, you dickhead!

NOELINE: Over the top? You think they're not being planned—

ROGER: Please can we try and keep this civil!

EMILY: [*to* NOELINE] Sometimes it's just kids talking big.

LISA: He is a dickhead!

ROGER: Lisa!

MICHAEL: That's always been the way she's treated me in case you've never noticed!

NOELINE: [*to* LISA] Our security forces aren't idiots! They know when a threat is real!

LISA: Poor, sad, little Michael. Sob, sob.

ROGER: [*loudly cutting through*] Michael's right! The dangers can't just be brushed aside. Australians have a right to be protected!

SUE: Roger, if our government really wanted to protect Australians, they'd be much better off spending the money mounting a concerted public education campaign to end violence against women. Violence perpetrated by rolled-gold, native-born, Liberal-voting, backyard-cricket-playing, Vic-Bitter-drinking, Australian men.

SABA: [*passionately*] Even if a few more refugees sail here, Noeline, does it really matter? Most of them are secular, who have fled Islam and the rule of the clerics. They're no threat to anyone!

SUE: Those poor souls on Manus and Nauru shouldn't be allowed to suffer because of a totally stupid belief that letting them come here will cause flotillas of malevolent terrorists to sail over the horizon.

NOELINE: It's cruel, I admit it's cruel, but if we let them come here I can guarantee you the floodgates *will* open—

> *At the trigger word 'floodgates' the room erupts into a confused roar of overlapping argument. Louder and more intense than the last.*

LISA: For Christ's sake, there won't be any floodgates—

SUE: There won't be any floodgates!

MICHAEL: Noeline's right! Thousands of them will start arriving and—

EMILY: Noeline, now you're being hysterical.

MICHAEL: No she's not!

EMILY: She is!

MICHAEL: There could well be terrorists among them!

SUE: Michael, don't be so ridiculous!

MICHAEL: I've always been—

LISA: Do you really think—

MICHAEL: —ridiculous as far as you're concerned.

LISA: Do you really think any terrorist—

NOELINE: [*to* EMILY] Hysterical? Now I'm hysterical?

SUE: That's not true. You're just being ridiculous right now!

LISA: Do you really think any terrorist would be—

ROGER: I'm not sure there'd be floodgates, Noeline, but—

LISA: —would be stupid enough to come here by boat!

NOELINE: [*to* EMILY] Hysterical!

MICHAEL: The policy is cruel, I'll admit that, and as—

NOELINE: If they do start coming again we're on the bloody frontline!

EMILY: Calm down, Noels! If a few more come we can cope!

SUE: Those poor souls have to be got off Nauru and Manus—

MICHAEL: And as a Christian that—

SUE: Got off Manus and Nauru as quickly as humanly possible.

MICHAEL: And as a Christian that doesn't sit easily with me but—

NOELINE: It's a harsh policy. I've said it's a harsh policy, but—

LISA: It's not just harsh, it's stupid.

SUE: It's insane. It's serving no purpose—

ROGER: All this shouting isn't going to get us anywhere!

SUE: No other purpose other than Duckett showing how tough he is!

LISA: How heartless he is!

EMILY: Even if a few more do come—Daniela's right. It's not the end of the earth!

NOELINE: Daniela's right and I'm wrong?!

LISA: What the hell would it matter if a few more did come?

NOELINE: [*shouting, upset*] It would matter to me! They're anti-woman, anti-gay and I just don't want them here! Okay, I just don't want them here!

There's a silence. EMILY *feels the need to apologise for* NOELINE's *outburst.*

EMILY: When she came out of the closet, her family disowned her—

NOELINE: You don't need to bring any of that up!

EMILY: I'm just trying to explain to them why you're so sensitive to anything anti-gay—

NOELINE: Well, don't.

EMILY: Her father still won't speak to her.

NOELINE: That's my business!

EMILY: She spent her life succeeding in a man's world to impress him—

NOELINE: Please!

EMILY: —and the minute she comes out he disowns her—

NOELINE: Just shut up!

LISA: Emily, she's a bully. Stand up for yourself for once in your little life!

EMILY: Lisa—

LISA: She's a bully. Stand up to her and don't be so gutless.

EMILY, *very upset, turns her back and moves away in tears.*

SUE: Lisa, no need to push it that far.

LISA: Sorry, sorry, sorry, but I am fucking well stressed! Dad, where are the keys!

SUE: Roger, give her the keys!

ROGER: No!

MICHAEL: [*to* ROGER] Don't give in.

ROGER: Michael—

MICHAEL: [*to* LISA *and* SABA] If your passion is that urgent, spend some money and go to a hotel.

NOELINE *moves across and tries to put her arms around a distressed* EMILY. EMILY *shrugs her off.*

NOELINE: I'm sorry. I'm upset. You're upset. This family is poisonous. It's time to leave.

ROGER: That might be best, Emily.

EMILY: So Lisa attacks me viciously, but I'm the one that has to go.

ROGER: I was just suggesting a possible solution.

SUE: Emily—

EMILY: Never be the third child. You get trampled on by your older siblings and totally ignored by your parents.

SUE: Emily, don't be so ridiculous.

EMILY: Ridiculous. That all the praise and all the kudos always went to the brilliant Lisa.

LISA: Shut up, for God's sake.

EMILY: Or to Michael whose Lego structures started to engulf the whole house to choruses of huge acclaim.

MICHAEL: Maybe I just might have deserved a little praise. I was four years ahead of my age in spatial visualisation.

EMILY: Whenever I tried to say something at the table Lisa just said, 'Shut up, stupid', and completely overrode me. And neither of you did anything to help.

ROGER: I continually told her to stop it.

EMILY: Yes, at least you tried, but not Mum!

SUE: [*hurt*] I did. Many times.

EMILY: I sure as hell can't remember. It was all about the wonderful Lisa! Lisa, Lisa, Lisa!

SUE: Darling you're imagining this!

EMILY: Do you know how I felt in those years? That it was a mistake I was ever born.

SUE: It may have been a surprise but not a mistake. You were greatly loved.

EMILY: Well, I never felt it. Not for one tiny instant of my life.

NOELINE: I've held her in my arms and listened to her sobbing for hours at the memory of it.

LISA: Oh migod. Where are the violins?

EMILY: I cried for a few minutes, Noeline. Don't bloody exaggerate.

NOELINE: As well as not knowing what I'm talking about, I exaggerate?

SUE: [*to* EMILY] We probably didn't pay you enough attention, but in our hearts—

EMILY: In your hearts? In your hearts? How was I supposed to bloody well know what was in your hearts when it never actually made it out of your mouths? All I ever heard was that Lisa was going to be a judge like her father, and that Michael with his phenomenal Lego skills was well on the way to becoming a ground-breaking architect like Frank Gehry. Frank Gehry? My God, Michael was so wedded to the right angle that the only thing he could ever have designed was a beachfront toilet block!

MICHAEL: I was accepted into Architecture—

EMILY: Until they saw your artwork folder and suggested town planning!

MICHAEL: I preferred town planning. It served a greater good.

EMILY: The most hated building inspector in Sydney because of your huge enjoyment of a little bit of authority. Known as Mick the Prick. When I used to try and borrow your Lego to make my own creations, you ripped them apart and said if I was going to do Lego I had to follow the instructions in those anal little coloured books.

MICHAEL: You dismantled my Lego Bulldozer, my Police Mobile Command, my Starfire One, my Alien Moonstalker, my Galaxy Commander—

EMILY: He remembers every one.

MICHAEL: Which might suggest how devastated I was.

EMILY: If you hadn't caught me I would've wrecked them all.

MICHAEL: My Galaxy Commander.

EMILY: It was the first time I felt really good in my life.

NOELINE: [*to* LISA *and* MICHAEL] You two put her through absolute hell.

LISA: Okay, I bullied, tortured and systematically turned my sister into a snowflake.

SUE: Noeline, there was sibling rivalry. There always is. Don't carry on. Let's have some cake.

NOELINE: Oh, I carry on as well?

EMILY: It was Lisa this, Lisa that, Lisa the all-time genius, and look at her now.

LISA: What's wrong with me now?

EMILY: You finally limped through an arts course repeating a year, got some nothing receptionist job at an ad agency, married the VP and you're now living off your overly generous divorce settlement and filling in your time with unpaid work worrying about people who've no right to be here in the first place. And having the gall to tell me my job isn't worth doing.

NOELINE: Come on, darling. You'll never get anywhere with these people. They ignored you when you needed love, bullied you whenever they felt like it, and now they're still belittling us.

SUE: Emily, I'm sorry you felt I ignored you. But perhaps—

EMILY: Perhaps what!

SUE: —if you felt that ignored you could have—

EMILY: What?

SUE: Sometimes you were as inscrutable as the bloody Sphinx. You could've been a little bit more assertive and let me know!

EMILY: [*flaring*] How could I ever be assertive in this family?! If I dared make a decision of my own, Lisa ridiculed it, you inferred it was wrong, and Dad lifted his eyebrow. Why do you think I was so lacking in confidence? This bloody family!

NOELINE: She has her own family now. Let's get out of here, pudding. This lot have caused you enough damage.

EMILY: I'm not going anywhere. It's Dad's birthday and he was by far the best of them. Talked to me when I was upset …

SUE: So did I, darling. So did I.

EMILY: Yes, but with you it always felt like 'Emily, you're making a mountain out of a molehill'.

SUE: I was dealing every day in my job with people whose lives were falling apart—

EMILY: So my problems were nothing in comparison?

SUE: I didn't say that!

NOELINE: Yes you did. I find it hard to believe a social worker couldn't pick up that she had a daughter who was being bullied by an overbearing older sister—

LISA: Oh migod.

SUE: How dare you?

NOELINE: And being teased at school day after day because she was shy, and being undermined by a brother who—

EMILY: Noeline, I can deal with this myself!

NOELINE: You mightn't have seen them as great problems, Sue, but Emily did.

EMILY: Noeline, butt out!

NOELINE: We should go.

EMILY: This is Dad's party. I'm bloody staying!

> *She plonks herself defiantly down on the sofa and* NOELINE *stands there, unsure of what to do, then decides that* EMILY *should be supported and plonks herself down too.* LISA *goes off to look for the keys.*

Actually you weren't that bad, Mum. Those two were worse.

SUE: Oh. So I was merely pretty terrible while they were rotten.

EMILY: I try and be honest and you bite my head off!

SUE: Believe it or not, I loved you and still do. I loved all of you. But at the moment I'm talking very much in the past tense because today's been a bloody nightmare. In future, family gatherings are right off the agenda!

ROGER: I'm sorry I suggested it. I had imagined we'd get together and reminiscence about the good times, completely forgetting that there weren't any.

NOELINE: [*to* ROGER] Did you know Lisa told Emily that she was adopted? And that she should run away because she wasn't really wanted?

SUE: Noeline—enough!

EMILY: Yes, for Christ's sake, shut up!

MICHAEL: Please stop using the Lord's name!

NOELINE: [*to* EMILY] They need to hear. Lisa told Emily she was adopted!

LISA: [*from the other side of the room where she's rummaging for the keys*] All older sisters do that.

NOELINE: And told her that Sue was dying of a rare tropical disease and soon she wouldn't have a mother, and she'd have to do exactly what Lisa told her.

EMILY: Noels, enough!

LISA: My God. You two must have a lovely time at night telling each other agony stories.

SUE: [*to* EMILY] You think you had it tough? I had an older sister who told me she had a bottle of deadly poison and was just waiting for the right time to put it in my food. I almost starved to death.

NOELINE: What kind of logic is that, Sue? It's alright for Lisa to have been incredibly cruel because there were sisters who've been even crueller?

ROGER: Enough! No more festering family grievances. And no more arguments.

SUE: Amen! Be civil to each other, and to me, or go home—all of you.

She pours herself a drink. Gulps it. ROGER *follows suit. There's a silence.*

EMILY *gropes for something to say that will return the gathering to a semblance of normality.*

EMILY: So. Daniela. Tell me a bit more about yourself.

NOELINE: Here we go!

EMILY: What do you mean, 'Here we go'?

NOELINE: You know what I mean.

EMILY: No, I don't. I was simply asking Daniela to tell me a little more about herself.

SABA: Really there's not much to— [tell]

NOELINE: You just can't help yourself, can you?

EMILY: Doing what?

NOELINE: Flirting. Flirting blatantly with every half-good-looking woman you meet.

EMILY: Noeline!

NOELINE: [*passionately angry*] Here I am defending you to the death against a family that turned you into a psychological basket case, and my reward is blatant flirtation right in front of my eyes!

SUE: [*a little drunk by now*] Emily?

EMILY: Yes, Mum?

SUE: I've seen sufficient of your new partner to offer just one word of advice.

EMILY: Which is?

SUE: Run.

NOELINE: [*to* SUE] Don't try and tell me I'm blind. Eyelids fluttering, little secret smiles. I know the routine.

EMILY: You're starting to really worry me, Noeline.

SUE: It's taken till now?

NOELINE: [*to* SUE] I breathe a sigh of relief when we get on board and there are six weeks when I don't have to worry about her eyeing off any woman in sight.

EMILY: If you keep being so bloody possessive, I'm not sure this marriage—

NOELINE: Oh, so if I ever mention your blatant flirting the marriage is off?

EMILY: You're paranoid.

NOELINE: We're going.

EMILY: Go. I'm staying right here.

NOELINE: You want to keep staring into the eyes of the sultry Daniela?

EMILY: Noeline. Daniela is hot. It's a fact. It doesn't mean I'm about to try and jump into bed with her.

SABA: And believe me I'm not about to jump into bed with *her*.

NOELINE: [*to* EMILY] I've put my whole career on the line for you. Time and time again.

EMILY: What?

NOELINE: We'll discuss it later.

EMILY: How have you put your career on the line?

NOELINE: You know damn well. I've covered up three blatant breaches of discipline at risk of my whole career.

EMILY: What?

NOELINE: If I was ever found out I'd be finished. And it'd be all over the press.

EMILY: I do my job perfectly well. What the hell are you talking about?

NOELINE: This isn't the time and place.

EMILY: If you're going to yell at me, do it now.

NOELINE: We'll talk about his later.

EMILY: No, let's talk about it now.

NOELINE: [*tough*] On three of our intercept operations you actively criticised Border Force officers for doing their duty.

EMILY: [*angry*] Doing their duty? Pushing, shoving, bashing and swearing at handcuffed men and women and locking them up in our hold!

NOELINE: They were illegals resisting orders.

EMILY: They weren't illegals. Of course they were resisting orders! They'd risked everything trying to escape a living hell and give themselves and their families a chance in life, then officers in *my* uniform called them scum. You really think they'd greet our guys with big smiles?

NOELINE: How else in the hell are we going to handle it? Go aboard their ships with champagne and canapés and tell them to look on the bright side of life?

EMILY: We don't need to behave like brutes!

NOELINE: We treat them as humanely as possible.

EMILY: Are you joking?! Lock them in dark, airless hold for over three fucking days and occasionally throw in some bottled water and muesli bars. A pregnant woman and kids? And when the woman's husband pleads that she's in distress she's finally allowed to see a doctor who tells her he's not allowed under Australian law to treat her and to drink more water!

NOELINE: If he had treated her it creates a duty of care and all kinds of legal complications!

EMILY: This is how a civilised country behaves to other human beings?

NOELINE: I didn't make the laws!

EMILY: Not content with putting them through hell on board we get to Indonesian waters and stuff them in a little, airless lifeboat with just enough fuel to get them to shore and cut them loose. And find out next day the fuel ran out and the only reason they're still alive is that there was an Indonesian fishing boat nearby!

NOELINE: We've stopped the boats!

EMILY: And lost our fucking soul!

> LISA *and* SABA *break into spontaneous applause. Joined by* SUE.

NOELINE: Why the hell did you apply for the job?!

EMILY: Because my marriage had gone to shit, I needed a job, and I swallowed the bullshit about serving our country and protecting our borders.

NOELINE: And the lives we've saved? That doesn't mean anything to you?

EMILY: Yes! I just hate how we're doing it!

NOELINE: Do you think I like seeing how those people are treated? I had no idea through all those years of training that this is what I'd end up doing.

SUE: What in the hell did you think you'd be doing?

NOELINE: Issuing warnings, sure. Rescuing people from sinking boats. Taking them for offshore processing. Not this!

LISA: Then get out!

NOELINE: And do what? I haven't got a divorce settlement or a rich family to bail me out! [*A passionate outburst*] I just do my bloody job! Get the boat where it has to go and get it back.

LISA: I'm just the train driver that drove the Jews to Auschwitz.

EMILY: That's not fair, Lisa. None of us knew what was coming when we signed up.

SUE: You know what's happening now. At some point you have to say enough!

> *There's a silence.* SUE *goes across and puts her arm around* EMILY. EMILY *accepts the gesture, burrowing her head into her*

mother's shoulder and shedding tears. ROGER *stands behind looking concerned but uncertain of what exactly to do.*

NOELINE: Please. This policy's not going to last forever.

LISA: It's lasted over six years already.

EMILY: Noels, you know how bad it is as well as I do. Not just for the refugees. For us. Three suicides amongst our officers just last year. It's horrible work.

LISA: Dad? Michael?

MICHAEL: [*angry*] I'm really hearing this for the first time. I had no idea we were treating them like that.

LISA: Well, how about you read a little wider than the truth according to Murdoch?!

MICHAEL: If that's what's happening to them—

EMILY: It is happening.

MICHAEL: —then it's wrong! As a Christian I can't condone it! I'm worried about Muslim extremism. Everyone is. But I don't condone that!

LISA: Are you going to do anything about it?!

MICHAEL: My church does recognise it's our Christian duty to welcome genuine refugees.

LISA: As long as they're Christians from Syria!

MICHAEL: We welcome everyone.

LISA: Has your church ever protested about Manus and Nauru?

MICHAEL: We joined an all-church delegation to request that children be taken out of the camps.

LISA: And the adults be left there to rot.

MICHAEL: Every week we pray for them.

LISA: Thoughts and prayers!

MICHAEL: We don't just pray. We go out of our way to welcome legitimate refugees.

LISA: Christians from Syria.

MICHAEL: Not necessarily.

LISA: Christians from Syria!

MICHAEL: [*agitated*] Alright! It is easier to be concerned about people of our own faith. We have social gatherings, barbeques.

LISA: Wow. Have a burnt sausage and become one of us?

MICHAEL: It's something!

SUE: Lisa, it *is* something.

ROGER: Yes, lay off your brother for just a second, will you?

LISA: [*to* MICHAEL] Would your church give sanctuary to a refugee who'd escaped detention?

MICHAEL: We can't break the law of the land.

LISA: Did it ever occur to your rigid authoritarian mind that your government may occasionally be morally wrong? A question that applies equally to you, Father.

ROGER: Lisa, there's no question that what's happening on Manus and Nauru is capable of being questioned morally—

LISA and SUE: [*together*] Capable of being questioned morally!?

SUE: Capable!?

ROGER: [*agitated*] I've upheld the law all my life! I won't break it now!

MICHAEL: And neither can our church.

SUE: 'I was only doing what my Führer ordered me to do!'

MICHAEL: Australia isn't Nazi Germany!

ROGER: No, it isn't, and to equate— lazy.

MICHAEL: As a Christian I don't like what's happening on Manus and Nauru, but what the hell am I supposed to do!

LISA: Show some guts. Break out of your obsessive rule-controlled brain for half an hour and finally become human!

MICHAEL: [*agitated*] Become human!

LISA: Become human! Throw away your Lego instruction books and do what a real Christian should do! Become fucking human!

MICHAEL: [*anguished, almost tearful*] Become—human! I've never been really human as far as you two are concerned. Okay, I'm different. I know I'm different! I did an online test years ago. Why am I part of that church you despise? Because I'm accepted. The first time ever in my life, because I certainly have never been accepted in this family! Except by Dad. Dad, who you all make jokes about because he doesn't spend his life searching for injustice—any injustice—so he can feel good about his righteous indignation! Thanks, Dad.

ROGER: Michael, your mother—

SUE: [*hurt*] I've always cared about you!

MICHAEL: You watched my sisters humiliate me all my life, Mum, and laughed along with them.

SUE: Michael, the girls occasionally had a joke. All sisters do.

MICHAEL: Joke? What they did to me in front of the first girl I ever took out was a joke?

EMILY: Yes it was.

>LISA *and* EMILY *look at each other.*

MICHAEL: You told her not to worry if I farted a lot as it only happened when I was anxious.

>LISA *and* EMILY *can't help smiling. Neither can* SUE.

LISA: And then you did!

MICHAEL: Because I was anxious! See, a big smile on your face. Like back then.

SUE: Okay. I'm not perfect! And yes, you were different. You were difficult. But believe me, I loved you and still do.

MICHAEL: I never felt it! Not once! It was always the girls with you.

EMILY: The girls? It certainly wasn't me. It was Lisa who was Mum's favourite by leaps and bounds.

>*This ignites a furious shouting match between the three siblings which is muddied, muddled, fast and loud.*

LISA: Will you both just fucking get over it!

EMILY: Easy for you, because you didn't—

MICHAEL: There you go. Pretending it didn't happen!

LISA: I am so sick of all your whinging! It makes me—

MICHAEL: It's just so easy for you to minimise—

EMILY: Bloody easy. You just swanned around in the glow of—

LISA: It makes me feel sick to hear all this pathetic—

EMILY: What's pathetic to you isn't to us—

MICHAEL: It's just so easy for you to minimise—

EMILY: You just swanned around in the glow of parental adoration—

MICHAEL: Just so easy to minimise what happened to me!

LISA: Jesus. My heart bleeds for you.

EMILY: Ridicule. Always your weapon.

MICHAEL: Yes, always ridicule—

LISA: Jesus fucking Christ!

MICHAEL: Unlike him, you never suffered—

LISA: Suffered! Why do you think I left my fucking marriage!

MICHAEL: Maybe he was sick of being married to a North Shore princess who—

LISA: Princess? Me, a princess?

EMILY: Of course you were a bloody princess. Still are!

> ROGER *finally can't stand it any longer and erupts.*

ROGER: Enough! Enough! It's bad enough turning seventy, but on top of that I have to witness the horror of my toxic genetic legacy!

> *Shocked silence.*

I used to endure the squalls of your childhoods by comforting myself that one day when I was old, my great consolation would be to be surrounded by mature, loving children. Instead I get an episode of 'Game of Thrones'!

> *More silence. All his children mutter 'Sorry Dad'.*

For just a few minutes can you behave like civilised human beings and pretend to enjoy each other's company?

> *His children mutter 'Sorry Dad' again.*

SUE: I think it's time for some cake.

> NOELINE *gets a message beep on her iPhone. She reads the message then turns.*

NOELINE: Daniela, you seem to know a lot about Iran.

SABA: Yes.

NOELINE: Where are you from, Daniela?

SABA: Why?

NOELINE: If it's Iran, I'm wondering how you got here. Iran doesn't allow emigration.

ROGER: Noeline, this is sounding uncomfortably like an interrogation.

NOELINE: It is. An alert just came though on my phone. An Iranian illegal called Saba Nazari skipped community detention and is on the run. And her description sounds very like you. And her photo looks even more like you.

SABA: [*finally unable to hold back*] Yes. My name is Saba Nazari. I'm from Iran. I am not Lisa's lover. It's been decided by Home Affairs that my psychological treatment for PTSD is over. When I heard this, I escaped detention. Because I did, Border Force can now deport me directly back to Nauru.

NOELINE: Justice Collins. You surely knew you have an obligation to report this to Home Affairs.

ROGER: I did. And have been debating what I should do.

MICHAEL: [*to* LISA] That's why you wanted the keys to the holiday house?

NOELINE: You were planning to spirit her to a hideaway? Which constitutes conspiracy to avoid legal deportation. Do you know what the penalty for that is, Lisa?

LISA: I'm doing what I have to do.

NOELINE: Ten years or a hundred and eighty thousand dollars.

LISA: Or both.

> NOELINE *takes out her phone and starts to dial.*

EMILY: What do you think you're doing?

NOELINE: Calling Border Force.

> EMILY *snatches the phone from her.*

EMILY: You'd send my sister to jail for ten years and think I'd still marry you?

NOELINE: She won't get ten years.

EMILY: Just five and a huge fine?

NOELINE: We can't encourage what your sister's done.

> *She fights* EMILY *to try and get the phone back.*

> EMILY *resists and to prevent* NOELINE *succeeding throws the phone to the nearest person. Her father* ROGER.

EMILY: Stamp on it, Dad. Wreck the bloody thing.

ROGER: I can't do that.

SUE: Wreck it.

ROGER: It would make me an accessory.

NOELINE: It certainly would. Throw it to me!

> ROGER *hesitates.* SUE *dashes across and swoops on it.*

[*To* SUE] You've actively preventing an officer of Border Force doing their lawful duty to apprehend a felon. You are now implicated.

SUE: A fugitive from justice. My life finally gets exciting!

ROGER: Darling, don't make matters worse for yourself. Give her the phone.

SUE: No way.

EMILY: I took the phone. I'm implicated too. You'd send me to prison?

NOELINE: Give me my phone. Now!

SUE: I'm not on board your bloody cutter.

NOELINE: Alright. You know what? I'm just going to sit here and watch you all dig yourselves in deeper. Go ahead. [*To* LISA] Leave with your felon if you want to. We'll catch you.

SABA: Justice Collins. You were a judge. Read those assessments of me by two independent and highly respected psychiatrists and see if you think I'm ready to be returned to the same place and the same conditions that caused my breakdown.

ROGER *picks up the assessments she gave him earlier.*

You don't have to read the details. Just the two summaries.

NOELINE: If the assessments are legitimate they would've been taken into account.

LISA: They weren't.

NOELINE: How do you know?

LISA: Read them. No-one with any shred of decency would send Saba back in her mental state.

ROGER *starts to read them.*

NOELINE: Mental state! You've got a broken leg, then fine. If you're feeling a little down, then pull yourself together and get on with life.

SUE: Actually, Noeline, in any other circumstance I might agree with you, but all I can see now is an ignorant, racist, closed-minded horror.

ROGER: [*looking up from the reports he's reading*] Sue, please—

MICHAEL: Noeline I know you're trying to uphold the law but in the case of Saba, sending her back if she's still seriously unwell does violate my Christian beliefs.

NOELINE: Join the lawbreakers then. It's on your head.

MICHAEL: I will. And I'll accept the consequences.

LISA: Thank you, Michael.

MICHAEL: The Lord guides me.

LISA: Hallelujah?

NOELINE: Saba give yourself up and don't make it tough for everyone. Nauru can't be that bad.

SABA: No? Then let me tell you. It's an ugly wreck of an island stripped bare of most of its vegetation by phosphate mining.

We are housed in mouldy tents. The heat is unbearable. You love the sun in Australia? We hate it. It is our enemy. We would love to

be able to rip it out of the sky. In Australia you do not allow pigs
to be housed like we are. Yes, we can go out into the towns, but so
many of us have been molested and harassed so we do it as little as
possible. We have barely enough money to buy enough food and
there are no fresh vegetables or fruit. And the hopeless feeling of
not knowing when this torture will end, of day after hellish day with
nothing meaningful to do, is unbearable. Your life has a purpose,
Noeline. Think of a life totally without purpose and with no future
hope of any purpose. Think of it. The thing that makes me angry,
so angry that it eats me from the inside, is that my life could easily
have had purpose. I could have been a doctor in Australia by now.
Before the mullahs declared that women should not pursue medicine any longer I had topped my year in medical school two years
in a row. I was outraged. I went out on the streets to join the democracy protests and was jailed and savagely beaten twice. I fled. And it
was hard and dangerous. Forged passports. Near— [rapes]. A leak-
ing boat, hugely overcrowded, large waves, fear we'd all drown,
seasick, hungry, thirsty, but in my heart huge hope. I was going to
the land where everyone is a happy neighbour like the Australian
television show I'd seen in Turkey on the way. But then we were
intercepted, yelled at, put on their boat, sat down on the deck, not
given food or water, and guarded. And instead of coming here and
finishing my studies what do I get instead? A guard who mastur-
bates openly at night while describing what he would like to do to
me. When I report him nothing ever happens because they say there
is no proof. It's hell. That's why I nearly killed myself. That's why
I probably will when I'm sent back. If I'd been allowed into your
country I might also one day be married with my own children.
Those are the dreams I still see in my head. Those are the dreams
that torture me and fuel my anger. Dreams that can never happen
because of your vile Mr Duckett! And you, Noeline, are about to
use your phone and send me back to that future with no hope and
no purpose.

There's total silence.

NOELINE: I don't have a choice.
EMILY: Border Force can go to hell. Saba is not going back to Nauru!

LISA *cheers and she and* SUE *hug* EMILY.

NOELINE: You're using the fact that I love you to blackmail me.

EMILY: Yes. Absolutely.

NOELINE: Ems, if it were just up to me I wouldn't send her back there either, but I'm here. In the same room as a fleeing deportee. Under oath I'd have to admit that. I'd lose my whole career. I have fought for it. I have overcome all kinds of prejudice. I have come from nothing and I have finally established myself. Throw away a whole lifetime of effort to get where I am? You can't ask me to do that! You can't.

SUE: No, we can't. Roger, we have reached a defining moment in our marriage.

ROGER: Susan, whatever you think you're going to do, you're not. Like Noeline, I have a lifetime of achievement to protect.

SUE: [*unleashing*] A lifetime of achievement! Upholding the law! [*Pointing to* SABA] The same law that's tortured Saba and hundreds of other poor souls for six years now?! All imprisoned in breach of the UN human rights charter!

    Beat.

If you want me to have any respect for you, going forward—I hate that phrase going forward—why did I just say it? If you want me to have any respect for you in the future, this is what's about to happen. Lisa will take Noeline's mobile phone and cleverly hide it under the pillow of our bed. And of course, Noeline, this is such a devilish place to hide it, that you'll take at least an hour to find it and Emily will testify that it took you both, as loyal Border Force officers, an hour of strenuous searching before it was located.

    ROGER *starts to interject but* SUE *plows on over him.*

Roger, you and I will drive Saba to a place I know of where Border Force won't find us, and we two will be the ones harbouring the deportee.

ROGER: [*alarmed*] Making us liable for ten years in jail or—

SUE: A hundred and eighty thousand dollar fine or both. Yes. Terrifying.

ROGER: God save me.

NOELINE: They'll find you.

SUE: It will take them a while, especially when Lisa tells them she over-heard us saying we were headed for the Blue Mountains. [*She turns.*] Actually—Roger, you go and hide the phone.

ROGER: It'll implicate me.

SUE: Exactly. Go and hide it.

SABA: It's no use Mrs Collins. They'll find us.

SUE: Eventually. But by that time all of the country's media will have received sound bites from my iPhone and have discovered that former Federal Court Judge, Justice Roger Collins, has made a hugely principled and courageous stand against the injustice of deporting psychologically fragile Saba Nazari back to Nauru.

ROGER: What?!

SUE: He has taken this courageous stand despite the advice of his reluctant wife Sue who fears the consequences of such a bold stance. But there was no stopping Justice Collins once he realised the enormity of the injustice.

ROGER: Having read the psychological reports it's certainly very, very wrong to send you back to Nauru but to defy the Government—

SUE: Justice Collins, his faced diffused with anger, said that after reading the psychological reports of the expert and totally neutral psychiatrists he was flabbergasted that any Government would even consider sending Saba back to an environment that would almost certainly provoke further suicide attempts—

ROGER: Are you going to tell me what to say?

SUE: Yes, word for word. I've been a black letter lawyer all my life, he said, but there comes a time, as was made clear by the Nuremberg trials, when a Government pursues policies that are so immoral that they can no longer be ignored, that any citizen of principle has to finally stand up and say I can't obey this Government any longer. There is a law that's higher and more important and that's the law of human decency, and this Government has traduced that law, and to hell with black letter thinking. I would rather face ten years in jail than bow down to evil!

ROGER: I'd never use language like that.

SUE: Until now. When the enormity of the injustice you witnessed freed your tongue at long last.

LISA: Bravo Dad.

EMILY: We're proud of you.

MICHAEL: Mum, I'd like to come with you. Hillsong isn't just about telling its congregation God wants them to get rich. We care.

SUE: That's very nice Michael, but let's not spread the risk too far.

ROGER: I won't do this.

SUE: Justice Collins then went on to say that Saba Nazari was a brilliant student who topped her first two years of Medicine in Iran. She was prevented from finishing her course by a cruel and repressive Clerical regime. She would benefit Australia by becoming a surgeon.

ROGER: I agree with all of that, but—

SUE: Justice Collins then challenged Mr Duckett to debate the issue on national television where he would reveal the devastating contents of the psychiatrists' reports.

ROGER: Do you want us to end our lives in prison?

SUE: We won't. By this stage you'll be a national hero and a celebrity. The Government will be hugely embarrassed. Pressure will be put on the Minister to allow Saba to stay.

NOELINE: Duckett won't back down.

SUE: He's rat cunning. He'll find a way that'll save his face.

ROGER: You can't force me to do this.

SUE: If you won't do it, I will. And there's much more chance that I'll end up in jail than you.

ROGER: You wouldn't.

SUE: Oh yes I would. And there's much more chance you'll be paying out a hundred and eighty thousand. My dear husband, we need your national profile.

EMILY: Come on Dad. Step up. Like the time you stepped up for me when I was being stalked. You went and confronted the creep head on and he was scary as hell.

ROGER: I was shaking for a month afterwards.

EMILY: But you did it.

MICHAEL: And the time you stood up for me at the football when that yob was threatening to bash my skull in.

ROGER: I was even more terrified after that.

MICHAEL: But you did it.

ROGER: That was for family.

LISA: Saba wants to become part of the Australian family.

EMILY: Dad. If you let Mum take all the risk, I tell you what, I won't be impressed.

NOELINE: [to EMILY] Don't encourage this!

MICHAEL: Dad, I'm your greatest supporter but in this case I'd also find it a little weak if you left it all to Mum.

ROGER: Et tu, Brutus?

MICHAEL: Where there is injustice, we must bear witness.

SUE: [*to* ROGER] Are you going to make me do this on my own? Or are you going to be part of it?

ROGER: What choice are you all leaving me?

SUE: Frankly, none. Hide the phone, or I will.

> SUE *goes and takes Noeline's phone from* LISA *and hands it out to* ROGER. *He resists taking it.* SUE *gets fed up and starts to move off with it.* ROGER *looks at the looks of disapproval of his children and lurches after her, takes the phone and disappears.*

> ROGER *returns to the room.*

ROGER: I'll have to pack some clothes.

SUE: No time.

ROGER: Underpants? Socks.

SUE: Let's move. Now. We'll find a Target on the way.

LISA: [*pointing at* NOELINE] She'll phone as soon as you leave.

ROGER: She won't be able to. If I'm going to do this I'm going to do it properly. I dropped it down the toilet.

EMILY: And she's not getting mine. Not for at least an hour.

NOELINE: I can't see clear evidence of the law being flouted and do nothing without being implicated! Can I, Roger?

ROGER: Noeline, the law works on the assumption, nearly always wrong, that people behave rationally. As a rational person, and hating the fact I disapprove of gay marriage, it's highly unlikely that you're even here today.

EMILY: And if you weren't here I wouldn't be as pissed off at you as I am now and our relationship would still be fine.

SABA: Noeline, it will cost your Australian taxpayers fifteen times as much to keep me on Nauru as here. You're doing your country a service.

NOELINE: I'm very uneasy about this—

EMILY: Are you here or not here! Just decide!

> NOELINE *makes a decision.*

NOELINE: Okay, I'm not here.

EMILY *hugs her.*

ROGER: Are you sure you know a place they won't find us?

SUE: Yes.

NOELINE: I have to warn you. It's not going to work. Duckett's stubborn as a mule.

LISA: We'll start an online petition. He's in a marginal seat.

ROGER: You're going to need a lot of signatures.

SUE: When your statements start grabbing the headlines we'll get them.

ROGER: I'm not being extreme.

SUE: Not extreme. Forceful. No evasive weasel legalese. No 'on the other hand' stuff.

ROGER: You'll all visit me in prison?

SUE: Duckett will back down.

NOELINE: Only if he can find someone else to blame.

SUE: Get the keys.

ROGER: The keys?

SUE: The car keys.

He starts to hunt for the keys.

ROGER: I'm sure I left them here.

SUE: Find the bloody keys!

He recommences his search.

ROGER: Where's this place we're going to hide that they won't find us?

SUE: In a hotel just across from Border Force headquarters in Canberra.

ROGER and LISA: [*together*] What!

NOELINE: No, good strategic thinking. Last place they'd look. But make sure when you send your sound files out that you hide the IP address by using a proxy server that diverts to another proxy server on a totally random basis. Not even Border Force can trace you if you do that.

SUE: How do you do that?

NOELINE: I'll show you. I'll write it to your notes app.

SUE *hesitates to hand her iPhone over.*

SUE: You just want it so you can ring Border Force.

NOELINE: How can I? I'm not here.

SUE *hands her the phone and* NOELINE *with great speed taps a set of instructions before handing it back.*

SUE: Roger, find the keys!

ROGER: When did I last take the car out?

SUE: Yesterday. To the supermarket.

ROGER: Ah, yes. To get the balloons.

MICHAEL: [*to* SUE] What was he wearing?

SUE: Darling, much as I'm fond of him I don't carry an indelible image of every change of clothes he makes.

ROGER: Do you think it was that red check shirt? And the fawn trousers?

LISA: [*chiming in*] And the fawn trousers?

SUE: I have no idea.

ROGER: It would help things if you could try and remember!

SUE: I think it was blue. The shirt. I can't remember the slacks.

ROGER: Half of my shirts are blue!

SUE: Which is why it was probably blue.

LISA: Did you put in in the wash?

SUE: I don't know.

EMILY: Well maybe look.

MICHAEL: Because if it's in the wash they could have disappeared into the crevices of that machine like they did a few months ago.

SUE: Your father is hopeless! Hopeless.

LISA: Are you sure you left them in a pocket somewhere?

ROGER: No I'm not! But it's a possibility.

NOELINE: Don't fart around for too long. There'll be computers whirring all over the country searching every electronic signal on any medium for the last twenty-four hours.

SUE: Okay. Noeline. Perhaps you could help?

NOELINE: I'm not here.

SUE: Could you all help! Please. All go and look in every drawer and every place you can think of. I'll go and look through his clothes. He once left his keys in the soap container in the shower.

Led by LISA, *all, except* NOELINE, *get up and start searching.*

EMILY: Noeline! Get off your arse.

NOELINE: I'm willing to assist passively but not actively.

EMILY: You've already told Mum how to evade electronic detection. Do you want me to tell them that under oath! Now get to it!

NOELINE *gets up and joins in the hunt, which becomes increasingly frantic.* SUE *reappears with a large bundle of shirts and pants and throws half of them to* LISA *and they both start sorting through pockets while the others look through drawers and cupboards all over the house. While this is happening we hear radio announcements that project us into the future.*

RADIO ANNOUNCER: [*voice only*] Australia has never seen anything like this before. A retired Federal Court judge risking a long jail term for making a stand on an issue he passionately believes in, sending messages by iPhone from a secret location believed to be somewhere in the Blue Mountains, where Justice Collins, his wife Sue and the refugee fugitive Saba, are evading a small army of Border Force officials. In case you missed it, this was his first announcement yesterday.

ROGER: [*voice only*] After reading the psychological reports of the expert psychiatrists I was flabbergasted that any government would even consider sending Saba back to an environment that would almost certainly provoke further suicide attempts. Saba Nazari was a brilliant student who topped her first two years of Medicine in Iran. She was prevented from finishing her course by a cruel and repressive clerical regime. She would benefit Australia by becoming a surgeon.

RADIO ANNOUNCER: [*voice only*] The might of Border Force versus Justice Collins. It's even started getting international attention. The *New York Times* editorial board commended the courage of Justice Collins in standing up to a law that is patently unjust.

ROGER: [*voice only*] I've been a black-letter lawyer all my life, but there comes a time, as was made clear by the Nuremberg trials, when a government pursues policies that are so immoral that they can no longer be ignored, that any citizen of principle has to finally stand up and say I can't obey this government any longer. There is a law that's higher and more important and that's the law of human decency, and this government has traduced that law, and to hell with black-letter thinking. I would rather face ten years in jail that bow down to evil!

RADIO ANNOUNCER: [*voice only*] Mr Duckett finds himself under increasing political pressure as a petition to let Ms Nazari stay already has over two hundred thousand signatures and the number is growing by the minute, helped by a statement from Saba herself.

SABA: [*voice only*] All I wish in life is to become an Australian. To contribute to your country and enjoy its freedoms. To one day marry and have children who can grow up secure in its freedoms. This is the dream I carry in my head. In my heart I hope that Mr Duckett might finally agree that I have suffered enough.

Onstage the frantic search for the keys continues. Suddenly ROGER *calls out.*

ROGER: Oh, hell!

Everyone stops and looks at him.

SUE: What?!

ROGER: They're in my pocket.

He pulls them out and shows them all. SUE *puts her head in her hands and groans.*

NOELINE: For God's sake, go! If Border Force crashes down that door and pours in it's not going to be much of a defence to tell them I'm not here! Go!

SABA: Yes. Please. Let's go! [*She turns to* NOELINE.] Noeline, at the moment the mullahs have interpreted the Quran to suit their own power interests. But brave Muslim women are challenging this. They have studied the Quran. There is nothing in it that says women can't work, can't have positions of authority, can't be President and speak their minds. At great risk to themselves they are changing Islam—I can see you are skeptical but this is happening. Very slowly but it is happening.

SUE: [*turning to her children*] I'm sorry I've been such a disappointing mother to you all, but when you reflect on all those traumas you went through at my hands, remember someone who had real traumas.

She points to SABA.

And don't be such bloody sooks!

ROGER, SUE *and* SABA *hurry out the door. We hear a car start up.*

NOELINE: [*to* EMILY] Get your things. We've got to get out of here.

LISA: [*to* EMILY] All that stuff.

EMILY: What stuff?

LISA: That we ignored you. It was true. Sorry.

MICHAEL: I'm not sorry. She wrecked my bulldozer, my police mobile command, my Starfire One, my Alien Moonstalker, my Galaxy Commander.

EMILY: Michael. I really am sorry about your Lego.

MICHAEL: Really?

EMILY: Yes.

MICHAEL: There's a vintage Lego website where you can still order those models.

EMILY: I'll get them.

MICHAEL: The Galaxy Commander is the one I'd really love to have again, but they're quite expensive.

EMILY: I'll get them.

LISA: [*indicating* EMILY] Michael. Feud over? She's done a great thing today. I'm proud of her.

> MICHAEL *nods and embraces his sister.*

NOELINE: Now you've done your huggies, can we please get going?!

EMILY: I'm ready.

NOELINE: [*as they start to leave*] I don't want too many of this bloody family at our wedding. Certainly not her.

> *She points at* LISA.

EMILY: She's coming.

MICHAEL: Actually, because of my beliefs I'd be unable to come in any case.

EMILY: You'll come or you won't get your Galaxy Commander.

NOELINE: Come on. We've got to go.

> NOELINE *and* EMILY *leave.* MICHAEL *turns to* LISA.

MICHAEL: I hope they don't end up in prison.

LISA: So do I.

MICHAEL: If they do it's your fault.

LISA: It's all of our fault. For letting this country become what it's become.

> LISA *leaves.* MICHAEL *shrugs and follows her. The stage is deserted.*

RADIO ANNOUNCER: [*voice only*] Breaking news. Mr Duckett is about to make a statement after consulting his colleagues and his department. We cross to Canberra now.

DUCKETT: [*voice only*] I make no apologies for the government's hard-line policy on refugees. It's stopped the boats and prevented drownings. But I'm not against using my ministerial authority when

I feel that humanitarian issues outweigh the strict letter of the law. I asked my department to delve further into this particular case and I found that regrettably, due to an oversight by one of my officials who has since been disciplined, the final two psychiatric assessments of Ms Nazari were not submitted to the relevant officers. When those assessments are taken into account I have personally determined that I will grant Ms Nazari, given her obvious ability to contribute to this country, and her proven rejection of religious extremism, a temporary visa which has the potential to be converted to citizenship after five years. Let no-one think however, that there will be any relaxation of the policy. This is a one-off case. I will do anything in my power to ensure no other refugee ever sets foot in this country.

Beat.

As for Justice Collins and his wife Sue, they have wilfully broken the law and will face the full consequences of their actions.

ROGER *and* SUE *enter their house after a final court hearing.* ROGER *is clearly disgruntled.*

ROGER: I get two hundred hours of community service and you get off scot-free! Why? I'm just a faithful wife.

SUE: You always said Justice Adams was a chauvinist.

ROGER: Look at this list. Picking up litter in our local park, painting the nearest community hall, scrubbing graffiti off public walls. Graffiti? In Pymble? Planting trees. For God's sake, round here you couldn't find one square metre where there isn't a tree!

SUE *has been looking over his shoulder and points to an item on the list.*

SUE: Hillsong's offering you a gig. Setting up and supervising community barbeques for Syrian refugees? [*Looking at him*] Better than picking up rubbish in the park.

She hands him a phone.

Ring your son, he'll be thrilled.

THE END

DAVID WILLIAMSON'S

FAMILY VALUES

DIRECTED BY LEE LEWIS

SBW STABLES THEATRE
17 JANUARY – 7 MARCH 2020

DIRECTOR
LEE LEWIS
DRAMATURG
VAN BADHAM
DESIGNER
SOPHIE FLETCHER
LIGHTING DESIGNER
BENJAMIN BROCKMAN
COMPOSER &
SOUND DESIGNER
STEVE FRANCIS
STAGE MANAGER
KHYM SCOTT

WITH
BELINDA GIBLIN
DANIELLE KING
ANDREW
MCFARLANE
JAMIE OXENBOULD
ELLA PRINCE
BISHANYIA VINCENT
SABRYNA WALTERS

Supported by
Government partners

NSW
Australian Government
Australia
Council
for the Arts

Special thanks

bangarra
DANCE THEATRE

Griffin acknowledges the generosity of the
Seaborn, Broughton & Walford Foundation in
allowing it the use of the SBW Stables Theatre
rent free, less outgoings, since 1986.

PLAYWRIGHT'S
NOTE

The genesis of *Family Values* happened some years ago when I turned on the morning news and heard the story of a Sri Lankan family with two small children, who had lived happily in Biloela for years, loved by their community, who were raided by Border Force at five o'clock in the morning without warning and told to gather what they could, then bundled off to detention prior to deportation.

I felt a wave of anger at the whole operation. It immediately made me think of the early morning raids of the most brutally repressive dictatorships in history, and made me alarmed at the sort of society we were rapidly becoming. Ramped up fears of terrorism, orchestrated by a Home Affairs department obsessed with saturation surveillance and control, had allowed the passage of some of the most repressive security legislation in any democratic country. Legislation given the green light by a Labor opposition terrified of being wedged as "soft on terrorism."

I started writing *Family Values* that same morning. It's not the story of that Biloela family, but of a psychologically damaged Nauru detainee who finds herself at the mercy of Home Affairs' Border Force, and also of a decidedly dysfunctional family.

From my earliest days as a playwright, as in *Don's Party* and *The Club*, I've loved to put people in the same room who are obliged to be together, but shouldn't be together, and don't want to be together. Humans being humans, this inevitably results in drama and comedy.

Much as the siblings in *Family Values* dislike each other, they can't not turn up to their father's birthday, and unfortunately for their father Roger and their mother Sue, things don't go smoothly, to say the least.

It has its comedic moments, as is inevitable when the members of that family straddle every fault line that's ripping at the heart of this nation.

But at its core it's asking the question: what sort of country have we become when we allow our Government to keep detainees indefinitely in wretched conditions without giving them any hope for the future, while using the totally spurious argument that repatriating them here will cause flotillas of Muslim terrorists to sail over the horizon and lay waste to our land?

David Williamson

DIRECTOR'S
NOTE

This is going to sound simplistic but bear with me. There is a huge difference between reading a play, thinking about doing it, programming it, casting it, seeing it in the season brochure, marketing it, giving interviews about it... and finally rehearsing it. And with a new play, no matter how much you've thought and talked about it, until you are standing in the rehearsal room with it in Week 2, you really have no idea what you are in for.

So standing in the middle of the rehearsal room in the basement of a tower in Barangaroo (kindly being shared with us by Bangarra Dance Theatre), I can say categorically that this is a miserable play to work on and I feel stupid for not having anticipated how hard it would be. Especially at this time.

It is Christmas next week. Sydney has been under a pall of smoke for six weeks as the country burns. The leadership vacuum has meant that neither the federal or the state government has provided any effective response to the crisis in either short term (being on the ground in threatened areas) or long term (addressing the demands of climate protests).That this is not surprising shows how inured we have become to inaction on the part of our leaders who are role-modelling wilful helplessness to a society with urgent problems, teaching us that change is not possible.

It is Christmas next week but Sydney isn't celebrating. Sure, the decorations are up, people are going to work with more sequins on than usual and you can't get a cab home at night because of the office parties. It looks like Christmas but the feeling is all wrong. You can't celebrate when your land is burning, when you've been at war for nearly twenty years, when the Uluru Statement From The Heart is ignored, while we continue to imprison human beings on Manus and Nauru. The weight of all the things we are getting wrong is accumulating. Sydney is usually pretty good at ignoring reality and leaping into summer holidays. But not this year.

This play is making the undertow of fear, anger, hopelessness and urgency obvious. David Williamson is doing the thing he has always done... putting his hands into our national wounds. In creating this family, he is showing us how dysfunctional the whole country has become. In creating these characters, the actors are having to dig around in the selfishness, the self-centred navel-gazing, the selfie-obsessed behaviours that dominate our thinking at the moment. At the heart of the play is great shame for who we have become.

There is also a sliver of hope in the play. That is perhaps David Williamson's defining characteristic as a playwright; his hope for humanity. He actually believes we can work our way out of the political, ecological and spiritual corner we have painted ourselves into. And at this time we need our playwrights to be offering a vision of a future that is not apocalyptic. The play in Week 2 is all in little bits on the floor; it is hard to see the hope. As we start to put it back together I know we will start to feel our way back to his instinct that we can't, as a country, give up on our values.

David is not letting Roger retire and play golf. He is making Roger use all the cultural capital he has accumulated in his career to fight the government's treatment of refugees. Ultimately David is using the final play of his extraordinary 50-year playwriting career as a protest. He is fighting for the future of civil society, for our capacity to work together to solve our biggest problems instead of trying to ignore them with chardonnay and tinsel. This play is not perfect but it is necessary. And it is an honour to stage his final statement at Griffin.

Lee Lewis

DAVID WILLIAMSON
PLAYWRIGHT

David is one of Australia's best known and most widely performed playwrights. Some of his 55 produced plays over the last 50 years include *The Coming of Stork*, *The Removalists*, *Don's Party*, *The Club*, *Travelling North*, *The Perfectionist*, *Emerald City* (including a Griffin production in 2014), *Money and Friends*, *Dead White Males*, *The Jack Manning Trilogy*, *Up For Grabs*, *Soulmates*, *Nothing Personal*, *When Dad Married Fury*, *Cruise Control*, *Rupert*, *Dream Home*, *Odd Man Out*, *Sorting Out Rachel*, *Nearer The Gods* and *The Big Time*.

Translated into many languages, his plays have been performed internationally, including in London (West End production of *Up For Grabs* starring Madonna), Los Angeles, New York and Washington (*The Club* in 1979 and *Rupert* in 2014 at the Kennedy Centre). David has adapted many of his plays into feature films, including *The Removalists*, *Don's Party*, *The Club*, and *Emerald City*, and has written many original feature screenplays including *Gallipoli*, *Phar Lap*, *The Year of Living Dangerously*, and *Balibo* (as co-writer) and for television he adapted *On The Beach*.

David's many awards include 12 Australian Writers' Guild Awards, five Australian Film Institute's Awards for Best Screenplay, and the United Nations Association of Australia Media Peace Award. David has been named one of Australia's Living National Treasures.

LEE LEWIS
DIRECTOR

Lee is the Artistic Director of Griffin Theatre Company and one of Australia's leading directors. For Griffin she has directed: *The Bleeding Tree* (Best Director at the 2016 Helpmann Awards), *First Love is the Revolution*, *Splinter*, *Prima Facie*, *The Almighty Sometimes*, *Kill Climate Deniers*, *Eight Gigabytes of Hardcore Pornography*, *The Homosexuals or 'Faggots'*, *Rice*, *Masquerade* (co-directed with Sam Strong), *Gloria*, *Emerald City*, *A Rabbit for Kim Jong-il*, *The Serpent's Table* (co-directed with Darren Yap), *Replay*, *Silent Disco*, *Smurf In Wanderland*, *The Bull*, *The Moon and the Coronet of Stars*, *The Call*, *A Hoax,* and *The Nightwatchman*. Other directing credits include: for Griffin and Bell Shakespeare: *The Literati*, *The Misanthrope*; for Bell Shakespeare: *The School for Wives*, *Twelfth Night*; for Belvoir: *That Face*, *This Heaven*, *Half and Half*, *A Number*, *7 Blowjobs*, *Ladybird*; for Hayes Theatre Co: *Darlinghurst Nights*; for Melbourne Theatre Company: *Gloria*, *Hay Fever* and David Williamson's *Rupert*, which toured to Washington DC as part of the World Stages International Arts Festival and to Sydney's Theatre Royal in 2014; for Sydney Theatre Company: *Mary Stuart*, *Honour*, *Love-Lies-Bleeding*, *ZEBRA!*; for Darwin Festival: *Highway of Lost Hearts*.

VAN BADHAM
DRAMATURG

Van is a writer, commentator, activist, occasional broadcaster, theatremaker and one of Australia's most controversial public intellectuals. As a playwright, her work has been performed across Australia and the UK, in the US and Canada, and in Iceland, Sweden, Switzerland, Italy, Slovenia, Germany and Austria.

She is the recipient of three Premier's awards for stage writing. She has been commissioned in Australia by Tasmanian Theatre Company and Melbourne Theatre Company, and in the UK by Luxi. In Australia, her works for stage and musical theatre have appeared at Griffin, Adelaide Festival, HotHouse Theatre, Malthouse, Merrigong Theatre Company and Terrapin Puppet Theatre. Internationally, her works have appeared at the Finborough, Edinburgh Festival, New York Summer Play Festival, Paines Plough, the Royal Court Theatre and Theatre503.

Her most recent theatre projects include *Banging Denmark* with Sydney Theatre Company. Her first novel *Burnt Snow* was published by Pan Macmillan in 2010. Her award-winning short film *Octopus* screened at the Dungog Film Festival, Tropfest Australia, Munich International Film Festival, Berlin International Film Festival and the LA Shorts Fest.

BENJAMIN BROCKMAN
LIGHTING DESIGNER

Ben is an award-winning lighting designer who works both nationally and internationally. Lighting design credits include: for Griffin: *Diving for Pearls*, *Replay*, *Splinter,* 2016 and 2018 Season Launches; for Apocalypse Theatre Company and Red Line Productions at the Old Fitz: *Angels in America Parts I & II*, *Metamorphoses*; for Bontom: *Chamber Pot Opera* (Adelaide, Edinburgh and Sydney Fringe Festivals); for Darlinghurst Theatre Company: *Broken*, *Detroit*, *The Motherfucker with the Hat*, *Tinder Box*, *Torch Song Trilogy*; for Ensemble Theatre: *Baby Doll*, *The Big Dry*, *Neville's Island*, *The Plant*, *Tribes*; for Hayes Theatre Co: *Razorhurst*; for KXT bAKEHOUSE: *Dresden*, *Jatinga*, *The Laden Table*, *Straight*, *Visiting Hours*; for Legs on the Wall: *Cat's Cradle*, *The Raft* (Development); for Mad March Hare Theatre Company: *Belleville*, *Bengal Tiger at the Baghdad Zoo*, *Dark Vanilla Jungle*, *Eurydice*, *Shivered*, *You Got Older*; for National Theatre of Parramatta: *Girl in the Machine*, *The Girl/The Woman*; for Shaun Parker & Company: *King*; for Squabbalogic: *Good Omens The Musical*, *Grey Gardens The Musical*, *Herringbone*, *Mystery Musical*, *Man of La Mancha*; for Spark Youth Theatre: *Political Children*; and for Unhappen: *Animal/People*, *Awkward Conversations with Animals I Have Fucked*, *Cough*, *Mr. Kolpert*. Ben's portfolio and upcoming productions can be found at benbrockman.com.

SOPHIE FLETCHER
DESIGNER

Sophie designs sets and costumes for theatre, film and television. Theatre credits include: as Designer: for Griffin: *A Strategic Plan*, *Caress/Ache*, *Emerald City*, *Gloria*, *The Feather in the Web*, *The Literati*; for Darlinghurst Theatre Company: *Broken*; as Co-Designer: for Belvoir: *This Heaven*; as Assistant Designer: for Melbourne Theatre Company: *Miss Julie*; for Sydney Theatre Company: *The Maids*, *Waiting for Godot*; and as Resident Props Buyer: for Sydney Theatre Company: *Arcadia*, *The Present*, *Speed the Plow*, *Three Sisters*. Film credits include: as Costume Designer: *Acute Misfortune*, *Angel of Mine*; in the Wardrobe Department: *Casting JonBenet*, *Holding the Man*, and *The Turning*. Short film credits include: as Designer: *Florence Has Left The Building*, *How to Get Clean*, *Measuring the Jump*, *Trespass*; and as Costume Designer: *Cattle*. Television credits include: as Costume Designer: for ABC: *The Letdown* and for Showcase: *Mr Inbetween*. Sophie is a graduate of WAAPA.

STEVE FRANCIS
COMPOSER AND SOUND DESIGNER

Steve has worked on over 100 theatre productions for Australia's leading companies as composer and sound designer. His theatre credits include: for Griffin: *A Rabbit for Kim Jong-il*, *A Strategic Plan*, *Between Two Waves*, *The Bull, the Moon and the Coronet of Stars*, *Speaking in Tongues*, *Strange Attractor*, *This Year's Ashes*; for Bangarra Dance Theatre: *Bennelong*, *Dark Emu*; for Bell Shakespeare: *Henry V*; for Belvoir: *Packer and Sons*, *The Sugar House*; for Legs on the Wall: *Man with the Iron Neck*; for Queensland Theatre: *Nearer the Gods*; and for Sydney Theatre Company: *The Battle of Waterloo*, *The Beauty Queen of Leenane*, *The Children*, *Disgraced*, *The Hanging*, *The Long Forgotten Dream*, *The Father*, *The Secret River*, and *Switzerland*. Steve has won two Helpmann Awards for Best Original Score for his work with Bangarra Dance Theatre on *Belong* and *Walkabout*. He has also won two Sydney Theatre Awards for Best Music and Sound Design, and was nominated for a Screen Music Award for his work on *Dangerous*.

KHYM SCOTT
STAGE MANAGER

Khym has previously worked for Griffin Theatre Company as Stage Manager for *First Love is the Revolution*, *City of Gold*, *Prima Facie*, *Good Cook. Friendly. Clean.*, *Kill Climate Deniers*, *Festival of New Writing*, *The Witches*, *Girl in Tan Boots*, *The Serpent's Table*; and for Griffin/Bell Shakespeare: *The Misanthrope*. Other recent credits include: for Belvoir/Malthouse: *Barbara and the Camp Dogs*; for Belvoir: *The Dance of Death*, *Miss Julie*, *This Heaven*; for Contemporary Asian Australian Performance: *Double Delicious*, *Stories Then and Now*; for Sydney Festival: *Lady Rizo: Red, White and Indigo*; and for Sydney Gay and Lesbian Mardi Gras. From 2013 to 2017, Khym was Assistant Stage Manager of The Australian Ballet, and toured with the company regionally, nationally, and internationally. Khym is a graduate of NIDA and The University of Sydney.

BELINDA GIBLIN
SUE

Belinda is one of Australia's most distinguished stage and screen actors. Her theatre credits include: for Griffin: *Dinner*, *Love Child*, *The Turquoise Elephant*, *Wicked Sisters*; for Adrian Bohm: *The Vagina Monologues*; for Apocalypse Theatre Company and Red Line Productions at the Old Fitz: *Doubt* (for which she was nominated for a Sydney Theatre Award); for Christine Dunstan Productions: *The Shoehorn Sonata*; for Christine Dunstan Productions and Company B: *Scam*; for Darlinghurst Theatre Company: *Daylight Saving*; for Ensemble Theatre: *Absurd Person Singular*, *Dark Voyager*, *Noises Off*; for Gary Penny Productions: *Steaming*; for Marian Street Theatre: *Canaries Sometimes Sing*, *Henceforward*, *How the Other Half Lives*, *Social Climbers*, *Things We Do For Love;* for Melbourne Theatre Company, Red Line Productions at the Old Fitz, Strange Duck Productions and Sydney Opera House: *Blonde Poison* (for which she was nominated for a Sydney Theatre Award); for Outhouse Theatre: *John*; for Perth Theatre Company: *Same Time Another Year*; for Playbox Theatre: *Quadraphenia*, *The World is Made of Glass*; for Queensland Theatre: *Blithe Spirit*; for Sport for Jove: *Ear to the Edge of Time*; and for Sydney Theatre Company: *Away*. Film credits include: *The Box*, *Demolition*, *The Empty Beach*, *Endplay*, *Liebe*, *On the Edge of the Bed*, *Peterson*, and *Say You Want Me* (for which she won a Sammy Award). Television credits include: for ABC: *MDA*; for Network Ten: *The Box*, *Heartbreak High*; for Nine Network: *Good Guys Bad Guys*, *The Sullivans*; and for Seven Network: *A Country Practice*, *Home and Away*, *Skyways*, *Sons and Daughter*.

DANIELLE KING
LISA

Danielle's theatre credits include: for ATYP: *Ishmael and the Return of the Dugongs*; for Bell Shakespeare: *Henry V*; for Christine Dunstan Productions: *The 98 Storey Treehouse*; for Darlinghurst Theatre Company: *Macbeth*; for Don't Look Away and KXT: *Night Slows Down*; for Moira Blumenthal Productions and Shalom: *The Man in the Attic*; for Outhouse Theatre: *4 Minutes 12 Seconds*; for Scrappy Assembly and Old 505: *Mercutio and the Prince of Cats*; for Sport for Jove: *Away*, *Hamlet*, *The Libertine*, *Macbeth*, *No End of Blame*, *The Taming of the Shrew*, *The Tempest*, *Twelfth Night*; for Sydney Theatre Company: *Noises Off*; and for White Box Theatre: *Blackrock*. Danielle's international theatre credits include: for the Almeida: *Coriolanus*, *Richard II*; for ATC: *Jeff Koons*; for Chichester Festival Theatre: *On The Razzle*; for Compass Theatre Company: *The Rivals*; for Northcott Theatre Company: *Two Gentlemen of Verona*; for Old Red Lion: *Simpatico*; for Sphinx Theatre: *As You Like It*; for the Studio: *The Art of Success*; for Theatre Royal York: *Hay Fever*, *Twelfth Night*; and for Young Vic: *Sleeping Beauty*. Film credits include: *Echo Pines*, *Felony*, *Fuse*, *The Gathering Storm* and *Hearts and Bones*. Television credits include: for ABC: *The Let Down*; for BBC: *Holby City*; for ITV: *Bad Girls*, *Ultimate Force*; for Nine Network: *Doctor Doctor*; and for Seven Network: *Home and Away*. Danielle trained at RADA.

ANDREW MCFARLANE
ROGER

Andrew has appeared in many of Australia's most admired films, television programs and stage productions. His theatre credits include: for Griffin: *Dreams in White*; for Black Swan State Theatre Company: *Arcadia*, *The Seagull*; for Ensemble Theatre: *Emerald City*, *Let the Sunshine*, *Losing Lois*, *Nothing Personal*; for Gordon Frost Organisation: *Fame*; for Melbourne Theatre Company: *Gulliver's Travels*, *The Heretic*, *Scarlett O'Hara at the Crimson Parrott*; for Queensland Theatre: *A Month in the Country*, *Cat on a Hot Tin Roof*, *Quartet*, *Who's Afraid of Virginia Woolf?*; and for Sydney Theatre Company: *Corporate Vibes*, *Cyrano de Bergerac*, *Mary Stuart*, *The Normal Heart*, *Woman in Mind*. Film credits include: *Born to Run*, *Boulevard of Broken Dreams*, *Break of Day*, *Doctors and Nurses*, *The Falls*, *Little White Lies*, *Razzle Dazzle*, *Returning Lily*, *The Shallows*, and *Truth*. Television credits include: for ABC: *Cleverman*, *Glitch*, *Janet King*, *Newton's Law*, *Patrol Boat*, *Play School*, *Pulse*, *Rake*, *Riot*, *Seven Types of Ambiguity*; for CBS: *The Code*; for Foxtel: *Miss Fisher's Modern Murder Mysteries*, *Secret City*; for Nine Network: *The Flying Doctors*, *Hyde and Seek*, *The Sullivans*; for Seven Network: *Between Two Worlds*; and for Showcase: *Return to The Devil's Playground*, for which Andrew won the 2015 ATRA Award for Most Outstanding Performance by an Actor. Andrew is a graduate of NIDA.

JAMIE OXENBOULD
MICHAEL

Jamie has worked in the performing arts for over 25 years. His theatre credits include: for Griffin Independent and Apocalypse Theatre Company: *The Dapto Chaser*; for Griffin and Bell Shakespeare: *The Literati*; for Bell Shakespeare: *The Miser*; for Cross Pollinate Productions and Red Line Productions at the Old Fitz: *The Village Bike*; for Darlinghurst Theatre Company: *Good Works*, *The Hypochondriac*; for Ensemble Theatre: *Baby Doll*, *Casanova*, *Last of the Red Hot Lovers*, *Neighbourhood Watch*, *The Spear Carrier*, *When Dad Married Fury*, *You Talkin' to Me?: Diary of an Olympic Cabbie*; for Mad March Hare Theatre Company and Red Line Productions at the Old Fitz: *Eurydice*; for Outhouse Theatre: *Trevor*; and for Sydney Theatre Company: *Macbeth*, *The Tempest*. Television credits include: for ABC: *Gasp!*, *My Place*, *Play School*; for Foxtel: *Secret City*; and for Seven Network: *Flipper & Lopaka*, *Oh Yuck!*. Jamie writes and directs short films that have screened at various film festivals including Adelaide Film Festival, Flickerfest, LA Shorts Festival, St Kilda Film Festival, Breath of Fresh Air Film Festival and Tropfest. His cartoons have recently been published in Meanjin.

ELLA PRINCE
EMILY

Ella's theatre credits include: for Griffin's Batch Festival and Sotto: *You've Got Mail*; for Bondi Feast and Sotto: *Arachnid*; for Bontom and Red Line Productions at the Old Fitz: *Chorus*; for Brevity Theatre and KXT: *A Girl is a Half-Formed Thing*; for KXT: *Rotterdam*; for NIDA and Sotto: *In a Year With 13 Moons*; for Old 505 and Sotto: *Safe*; for Red Line Productions at the Old Fitz and White Box Theatre: *The Shadow Box*; and for Red Line Productions at the Old Fitz and Workhorse Theatre Company: *4.48 Psychosis*. Film credits include *Foreclosure*, *Interface*, *Last Night*, *Mazi Sou*, *Star Dust* and *Wall Space*. As a writer, Ella's work includes *Arachnid* for Bondi Feast and Sotto, *Finch: Love Addict* for Sotto and *Eli's Winter* for AFTRS. Ella trained at RADA.

BISHANYIA VINCENT
NOELINE

Bishanyia's theatre credits include: for Griffin Independent and Bali Padda: *Lighten Up*; for Darlinghurst Theatre Company: *The Rise and Fall of Little Voice*; for Ensemble Theatre: *The Last Wife*; for Hayes Theatre Co: *Evie May*, *Spamalot*; for KXT and Lies Lies and Propaganda: *A Christmas Carol*; for New Theatre: *Harvest*, *The HIV Monologues*, *Nell Gwynn*, *Top Girls*; for Red Line Productions at the Old Fitz: *Where Do Little Birds Go?*, *The Wind in the Underground*; for Sport for Jove: *One Flew Over the Cuckoo's Nest*; and for Squabbalogic: *The Dismissal*. Bishanyia's international theatre credits include: for Blenheim Palace Gardens: *As You Like It*; for Eastern Angels: *Private Resistance*; for Hampstead Theatre: *After The Fall*, *Selling Me*; for OSD Theatres: *The Country Wife*, *The Mother in Law*, *Othello*, *Time and the Conways*; and for Theatre Royal Haymarket: *The Rivals*. Television credits include: for ABC: *#7DaysLater*, *The Strange Chores*; for Cheeky Little Media: *Monster Teddies*: for Netflix: *Motown Magic*; for Netflix and Seven Network: *Beat Bugs*; for Nickelodeon: *Blair and Sea Pancake*; and for Seven Network: *Jay's Jungle*. Bishanyia trained at the Oxford School of Drama and is a proud member of MEAA.

SABRYNA WALTERS
SABA

Sabryna's theatre credits include: for Griffin: *Caress/Ache*; for Bell Shakespeare: *Macbeth*; for Genesian Theatre: *Saint Joan*; for Mad March Hare Theatre Company: *A Moment on the Lips*; for Merrigong Theatre Company: *Dead Man Brake*; for NIDA: *A Midsummer Night's Dream*, *Flight*, *Rare Earth*, *Twelfth Night*; and for Sport for Jove: *Hamlet*, *Love's Labour's Lost*, *Romeo and Juliet*. Television credits include: for Foxtel: *The Fighting Season*. Short film credits include *Staircase*, *The Armageddon Code*, and *Ordinary*. Sabryna is a graduate of NIDA.

ABOUT GRIFFIN

Griffin is the only theatre company in the country entirely devoted to producing new Australian plays. Located in the historic SBW Stables Theatre, nestled in the heart of bustling Kings Cross, Griffin has been a permanent home for the exploration of Australian stories since 1978.

Many of this country's most beloved and celebrated artists started out on our stage— Cate Blanchett, Michael Gow, Louis Nowra, David Wenham, to name a few—and iconic Australian plays like *The Boys*, *Holding the Man* and *The Bleeding Tree* had their world premieres at Griffin, before going on to capture the national imagination. We are a theatre of first chances.

We are passionate about nurturing emerging artists. We help ambitious, bold, risk-taking and urgent Australian plays get from a page onto a stage. We tell the stories that will help us know who we are as a nation, and who we want to become.

Stories about us. Written by us. For us.

GRIFFIN THEATRE COMPANY
13 Craigend St
Kings Cross NSW 2011
02 9332 1052
info@griffintheatre.com.au
griffintheatre.com.au

SBW STABLES THEATRE
10 Nimrod St
Kings Cross NSW 2011

BOOKINGS
griffintheatre.com.au
02 9361 3817

GRIFFIN FAMILY

PATRON

Seaborn Broughton
& Walford Foundation

Griffin acknowledges the generosity of the Seaborn, Broughton & Walford Foundation in allowing it the use of the SBW Stables Theatre rent free, less outgoings, since 1986.

BOARD

Bruce Meagher (Chair)
Simon Burke AO
Lyndell Droga
Tim Duggan
Lee Lewis
Mario Philippou
Julia Pincus
Lenore Robertson
Karen Rodgers
Simone Whetton
Meyne Wyatt

ARTISTIC

**Artistic Director
& CEO**
Lee Lewis
Artistic Associate
Phil Spencer

ADMINISTRATION

Executive Director
Karen Rodgers
Associate Producer, Development
Frankie Greene
Associate Producer, Marketing
Estelle Conley
Associate Producer, Programming
Imogen Gardam
Marketing Coordinator
AJ Lamarque
Development Coordinator
Ell Katte
Communications Coordinator
Ang Collins
Program & Administration Coordinator
Whitney Richards
Strategic Insights Consultant
Peter O'Connell

PRODUCTION

Production Manager
Ryan Garreffa
Production Coordinator
Dana Spence

FINANCE

Finance Consultant
Tracey Whitby
Finance Manager
Kylie Richards

CUSTOMER RELATIONS

Box Office Manager
Dominic Scarf
Bar Manager
Grace Nye-Butler
Customer Relations Team
Ell Katte
Julian Larnach
Janine Ledet
Poppy Tidswell

GRAPHIC DESIGN
Alphabet

COVER PHOTOGRAPHY
Brett Boardman

GRIFFIN DONORS

Income from Griffin activities covers less than 40% of our operating costs—leaving an ever increasing gap for us to fill through government funding, sponsorship and the generosity of our individual supporters. Your support helps us bridge the gap and keep ticket prices affordable and our work at its best. To make a donation and a difference, contact Griffin on **9332 1052** or donate online at **griffintheatre.com.au**

COMPANY PATRONS
Merilyn Sleigh
& Raoul de Ferranti

PRODUCTION PATRON
Girgensohn Foundation

PROGRAM PATRONS
Griffin Ambassadors
Robertson Foundation

Griffin Studio
Gil Appleton
Darin Cooper Foundation
Ken & Lilian Horler
Kiong Lee & Richard Funston
Pip Rath & Wayne Lonergan
Malcolm Robertson
Foundation
Geoff & Wendy Simpson
Danielle Smith
Walking up the Hill
Foundation

Griffin Women's Initiative
Griffin Women's Initiative
is supported by Creative
Partnerships Australia
through Plus1

Katrina Barter
Wendy Blacklock
Christy Boyce &
Madeleine Beaumont
Laura Crennan
Lyndell Droga
Melinda Graham
Sherry Gregory
Antonia Haralambis
Ann Johnson
Roanne Knox
Julia Pincus
Ruth Ritchie
Lenore Robertson
Sonia Simich
Margie Sullivan
Simone Whetton

PRODUCTION PATRONS
As a new writing theatre,
we program a wide range of
stories that reflect our time,
place and the unique voice
of contemporary Australia.
To ensure that these stories
continue to be told, Griffin
needs the help of private
support to bring strength,
insight, candour and new
and powerful visions to
the stage. Our Production
Partner program is vital to our
continued artistic success.

Kindness by Matthew Whittet
Darin Cooper Foundation

Prima Facie by Suzie Miller
Robert Dick & Erin Shiel
Richard McHugh
& Kate Morgan
Andrew Post & Sue Quill
Richard Weinstein
& Richard Benedict

City of Gold by Meyne Wyatt
Andrew Cameron AM & Cathy
Cameron
Bruce Meagher & Greg Waters
Julia Pincus & Ian Learmonth
Malcolm Robertson
Foundation
David Marr &
Sebastian Tesoriero
The Sky Foundation
Kim Williams AM and
Catherine Dovey
Ann & Brian O'Connell (in
memoriam)

Splinter by Hilary Bell
Stephen Fitzgerald

SEASON DONORS
Front Row Donors +$10,000
Andrew Cameron AM &
Cathy Cameron
Darin Cooper Foundation
Robert Dick & Erin Shiel
Stephen Fitzgerald
The Girgensohn Foundation
Belinda Hazelton & Vicki Archer
Ingrid Kaiser
Malcolm Robertson Foundation
Richard McHugh &
Kate Morgan
Peter & Dianne O'Connell
Rebel Penfold-Russell
Julia Pincus & Ian Learmonth
Pip Rath & Wayne Lonergan
Robertson Foundation
The Sky Foundation
Merilyn Sleigh &
Raoul de Ferranti
Kim Williams AM &
Catherine Dovey

Main Stage Donor
$5,000 - $9,999
Anonymous (1)
Ellen Borda
Wendy Blacklock
Louise Christie
Lyndell & Daniel Droga
Danny Gilbert AM &
Kathleen Gilbert
Helen & Abraham James &
Family
Kiong Lee & Richard Funston
Lee Lewis & Brett Boardman
David Marr &
Sebastian Tesoriero
Sophie McCarthy &
Antony Green
Bruce Meagher & Greg Waters
Don & Leslie Parsonage
Sue Procter
Geoff & Wendy Simpson
Danielle Smith

GRIFFIN DONORS

Final Draft $2,000-$4,999

Gae Anderson
Baly Douglass Foundation
Lisa Barker & Don Russell
Helen Bauer &
Helen Lynch AM
Marilyn & David Boyer
Bernard Coles
Alan Colletti
Bryony & Tim Cox
Lachlan Edwards
Gordon & Marie Esden
Elizabeth Fullerton
Kathy Glass
Libby Higgin
Roanne & John Knox
Carina G. Martin
John McCallum & Jenny Nicholls
John Mitchell
Catriona Morgan-Hunn
David Nguyen
Anthony Paull
Chris Reed
Leslie Stern
Stuart Thomas
Tea Uglow
Richard Weinstein &
Richard Benedict

**Workshop Donor
$1,000-$1,999**

Anonymous (3)
Brian Abel
Antoinette Albert
Andrew Bell & Joanna Bird
Cherry & Peter Best
Keith Bradley AM
Michael & Charmaine Bradley
Dr Bernadette Brennan
Jane Bridge
Corinne & Bryan
Iolanda Capodanno
Peter Chapman
Sally Crawford
Nathan Croft & James White
Cris Croker & David West
Jane Curry
Timothy Davis
Carol Dettmann
Christine Dunstan
Ros & Paul Espie
Brian Everingham
John & Libby Fairfax

Rowena Falzon
Robyn Fortescue &
Rosie Wagstaff
Jennifer Giles
Peter Gray & Helen Thwaites
Reg Graycar
Judge Joe Harman
James Hartwright &
Kerrin D'Arcy
John Head
Danielle Hoareau
Mary Holt
Mark Hopkinson &
Michelle Opie
Ann Johnson
Margaret Johnston
David & Adrienne Kitching
Jennifer Ledgar & Bob Lim
Richard & Elizabeth Longes
Elaine & Bill McLaughlin
Dr Steve McNamara
Kent & Sandra McPhee
Joy Minter
Kate Mulvany
Tommy Murphy
Ian Neuss
Patricia Novikoff
Ian Phipps
Martin Portus
Steve & Belinda Rankine
Steve Riethoff
Annabel Ritchie
Sylvia Rosenblum
Mary Ann Rolfe
Jann Skinner
Geoffrey Starr
Robyn Stone
Adam Suckling &
Pip McGuinness
Augusta Supple
Peter Talbot
Mike Thompson
Sue Thomson
Daniel P. Tobin
Ariadne Vromen
Janet Wahlquist
Simone Whetton
Paul & Jennifer Winch
Elizabeth Wing
Kathy Zeleny

Reading Donor $500-$999

Anonymous (1)
Jes Andersen
Robyn Ayres
Melissa Ball
Michael Barnes
Nikki Barrett
Phillip Black
Annie Bourke
Rebecca Bourne Jones
Anne Britton
Simon Burke AO
Bill Calcraft
Gaby Carney
Michael Diamond
Max Dingle
Susan Donnelly
Tim Duggan
Wendy Elder
Bob Ernst
Nicky Gluyas
Peter Graves
Tonkin Zulaikha Greer
Edwina Guinness
Con & Antonia Haralambis
Stephanie & Andrew Harrison
David Hoskins & Paul McKnight
Sylvia Hrovatin
Susan Hyde
Marian & Nabeel Ibrahim
Mira Joksovic
Maruschka Loupis
Anne Loveridge
Ian & Elizabeth MacDonald
Chris Marrable
Christopher McCabe
Wendy McCarthy AO
Patrick McIntyre
Nicole McKenna
Paula McLean
Neville Mitchell
Alex Oonagh Redmond
Judith & Frank Robertson
Carolyn Penfold
Judy Phillips
Malcolm Poole
Roslyn Renwick
Karen Rodgers & Bill Harris
Gemma Rygate
Rob & Rae Spence
Mary Stollery & Eric Dole

GRIFFIN DONORS

Catherine Sullivan &
Alexandra Bowen
Pearl Tan & Priya Roy
Elizabeth Thompson
Jonathan Ware
John Waters
Rosemary White

First Draft Donor $200-$499
Anonymous (5)
Nicole Abadee & Rob
Macfarlan
Susan Ambler
Wendy Ashton
Penny Beran
Edwina Birch
Shay Bristowe
Peter Brown
Dean Bryant & Mathew Frank
Wendy Buswell
Ruth Campbell
David Caulfield
Charlie Chan &
Angela Catterns
Peter Chapman
Sue Clark
Bryan Cutler
Joanne & Sue Dalton
Owen Davies
Dora Den Hengst
Dr June Donsworth
Peter Duerden
Michele Dulcken
Elizabeth Evatt
Paul Fletcher
Lee French
Matt Garrett
Sarah & Braith Gilchrist
Deane Golding
Brenda Gottsche
Jennifer Hagan & Ron Blair

Elizabeth Hanley
Carol Hargreaves
Matthew Huxtable
Susan J Kath
C John Keightley
Penelope Latey
Peta Leemen
Antoinette Le Marchant
Liz Locke
Dr Peter Louw
Carolyn Lowry
Anni MacDougall
Robert Marks
Guillermo Martin
Edward McGuiness
Duncan McKay
Ian McMillan
Sarah Miller
Sarah Mort
Mullinars Casting
Consultants
Dian Neligan
Carolyn Newman
Gennie Nevinson & Vivian
Manwaring
Anthony Ong
Peter Pezzutti
Meredith Phelps
Belinda Piggott & David
Ojerholm
Marion Potts
Christopher Powell
Andrew Pringle
Virginia Pursell
Thelma Roach
Ann Rocca
Catherine Rothery
David & Dianne Russell
Kevin and Shirley Ryan
Sharryn Ryan

Julianne Schultz
Julia Selby
Diana Simmonds
Vanda and Martin Smith
The Steiner Family
Camilla Strang
Stephen Thompson
Deanne Weir
Jennifer White
Ruth Wilson
Eve Wynhausen
William Zappa
Aviva Ziegler

*We would also like to thank
Peter O'Connell for his
expertise, guidance and time.*

Current as of 25 November
2019

SPONSORS

Government Supporters

Australia Council for the Arts
Australian Government

NSW Government

Patron

2020 Season Sponsor

alphabet.

Production Partner

GIRGENSOHN
FOUNDATION

Griffin Studio & Griffin Award

CULTURAL FUND
COPYRIGHT AGENCY

Griffin Studio

MALCOLM ROBERTSON FOUNDATION

Griffin Ambassadors &
Artistic Associate Sponsor

ROBERTSON FOUNDATION

Company Lawyers

MARQUE

Associate Sponsor

Brett Boardman Photography

Company Sponsors

SATURDAY PAPER

THE UNIVERSITY OF SYDNEY
PERFORMANCE STUDIES

Rosenfeld, Kant & Co.
Business & Financial Solutions

MOPPITY

CURRENCY PRESS

Coopers

FOUR PILLARS

bourke street bakery

Access Partners

DESIGNKINGCOMPANY

Griffin Theatre Company is assisted by the Australian Government through the Australia Council, its arts funding and advisory body; and the NSW Government through Create NSW.

www.ingramcontent.com/pod-product-compliance
Lightning Source LLC
Chambersburg PA
CBHW040055100426
42734CB00044B/3404